WELL VERSED 2022

COLUMBIA CHAPTER OF THE
MISSOURI WRITERS GUILD

D1570496

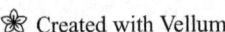 Created with Vellum

CONTENTS

FICTION

NONFICTION

FORWARD BY PRESIDENT

In the last year the Columbia Writer's Guild—and the world—transitioned from being sheltered and cautious to opening back up, meeting in person, and hoping the worst is behind us. The prose and poetry in Well Versed 2022 reflects this determination to overcome the struggles and challenges of our new reality, while the fictional stories let us escape for a while into different places and other worlds.

I'd like to thank all those who made Well Versed 2022 possible: our contributors, volunteers, and judges. A special thanks to our managing editor, Marsha Posz, for working diligently on Well Versed. This is her last year as editor, and she will be missed. I'd also like to thank our treasurer, Charles Tutt, for handling the money aspects, and Anne Gifford for organizing the Summer Flash Fiction contest each year. All the hard work has paid off, yielding another stirring edition of Well Versed.

I hope you find something within these pages to inspire you.

Deb Sutton
CCMWG Presiden

EDITOR'S NOTE

This year we asked CWG Members to submit their photos and art for a chance to be on the cover or in Well Versed 2022. We receive some truly amazing submissions, making it difficult to choose. In the end we went with the simplicity and beauty of A Wish by Lisa Adams-Lloyd. As you read through this years anthology take note of the photos and art included.

I'm again encouraged by the submissions this year. The members of CWG and other contributors have stepped forward and brought us this rich and diverse anthology. Our launch will again be in person as we bring the 2022 season of *Well Versed* to a close. I thank each of you for your submissions and contributions. I would also like to thank our peer readers and judges for their time in reading the large number of submissions we processed this year. Thanks to Anne Gifford for making the Summer Flash Fiction contest possible. It is always enjoyable and I know everyone looks forward to it. Thanks to Charles Tutt for keeping track of the current members list and handling questions about ordering, address changes, and the financial aspects of our anthology. Lastly, thanks to Deb Sutton for leading us and helping me with aspects of the editing process. Deb does a lot behind the scenes of *Well Versed* and I appreciate all her efforts.

This is my last year of Well Versed as I am stepping down as your editor-in-chief. I appreciate everyone's support. It wasn't an easy decision to make. As the CWG looks forward to another year, I wish you all the best and have no doubt next year's anthology will be just as inspiring!

Marsha Posz
Editor, *Well Versed 2021*

Glendaloch by Terry Allen

POETRY

Photo credit: Terry Allen

POETRY JUDGE

Walter Bargen

Walter Bargen has published 25 books of poetry. Recent books include: *Days Like This Are Necessary: New & Selected Poems* (BkMk Press, 2009), *Trouble Behind Glass Doors* (BkMk Press, 2013), *Perishable Kingdoms* (Grito del Lobo Press, 2017), *Too Quick for the Living* (Moon City Press, 2017), *My Other Mother's Red Mercedes* (Lamar University Press, 2018), *Until Next Time* (Singing Bone Press, 2019), *Pole Dancing in the Night Club of God* (Red Mountain Press, 2020), and *You Wounded Miracle*, (Liliom Verlag, 2021). His awards include: a National Endowment for the Arts Fellowship, Chester H. Jones Foundation Award, and the William Rockhill Nelson Award. He was appointed the first poet laureate of Missouri (2008-2009).

THE BUTTAHACHEE RIVER BOOK CLUB

TERRY ALLEN

We're pleased to announce
these three final choices
for our annual community book read.
Remember to vote now and vote often
for your favorite from the list below:

1.

Hugh Langstaff has done it again
with his latest Beefcake Romance,
Small Town Grease Monkey Daddy,
which turns out to be a stellar addition
to his popular series:
Small Town Minister's Wife,
Small Town Biker Queen,
and *Small Town Car Hop Hunk.*
Expect the unexpected in this wonderfully
irreverent view of small town life,
filled with Southern Gothic eccentrics

that rivals anything written by Eudora Welty.
If you like grotesque characters
and dark humor, this book is for you!

2.

Eileen Kinsman's remarkable social satire
in the full glory of iambic pentameter,
I'd Rather Do It Myself, If You Don't Mind,
is a delight to read and remember,
beginning with the freakish encounter
of a therapist, a priest and a grocery clerk
who walk into a bar together
and find it's "Achy Breaky Heart Night."

3.

The Ghostly Spirit at Your Momma's Wake
is Rosemary Newman's new novel
about the paranormal, or I should say,
her first posthumously published phantasm.
Sadly, Kate appears to have vanished
and has not been seen since that "encounter"
that inspired this frightening work,
or we should say, led to her mental breakdown
following that unfortunate skirmish
with three black cats and a groundhog.

Postscript:

As president of the Buttahachee River Book Club,
I'd just like to add a personal note that one
of this year's nominees did not make the final list,
but was a big favorite. So, here's a special

shoutout to Chandler Poole's new biography about that prodigious author, cartoonist, illustrator, poet, and animator Theodor Geisel, entitled *Dr. Seuss Hears a Horton.*

CONTRADICTORY WORLDS

MARCIE MCGUIRE

In the first world, a woman stands on a bluff
overlooking the creek that flows through town, watching
a red-tailed hawk circle the woods below, wondering
whether she should see the artist again.
He is filled with passion. He carries a heavy burden.
They could make each other miserable. She thinks
she will distract him from his work. He will resent her.
She decides not to see him again. Instead, she
reupholsters her chairs and alphabetizes her spices.
She buys watercolors and learns to paint translucent
panes, light and shadows, reflections upon water.
Years pass and she thinks of him less often. She
attends exhibits and sees his work in town. Sometimes
she recognizes a familiar gesture, senses his
steady strokes carrying him surely over deep waters.

In the second world, she decides to see him again. She
kisses the back of his neck, and he turns toward her.
They make love eagerly, on the couch in his studio
or outside beneath the trees. They push aside the dishes

and make love on the table. They are obsessed. They
cannot get enough. They do not see the shadows moving
across their bed. One morning they get up and argue
about the dirty pans that someone left in the sink. She
picks up the laundry and vacuums the floor. He carries
sacks of aluminum cans and newspapers out for
recycling. She suggests they put plastic over their windows.
He looks at the wood pile and calculates the fires that
remain. They are filled with immeasurable sadness.

In the third world, she decides to see the artist again.
He is filled with passion. He carries a heavy burden.
He drags her through his darkest nights. She
pushes him right to the edge, distracts him from his work.
He cranks the volume up and forces the paint to
sing down steep canyons. Strange shapes rise within him,
fleeting shadows move across his face. He wants her
to see what he saw, in late winter, when he stood
behind her, his hands on her shoulders, over the creek
where a red-tailed hawk floated on updrafts—
the shapes, the textures, the way light moved across the rocks,
how the back of her head fit precisely into his hand.
He kisses her neck, and she turns toward him.
He presses his fingers against the base of her spine,
and they move steadily against strong currents.

LORD HAVE MERCY

MARCIE MCGUIRE

The day the bishop was buried, in rain and
freezing drizzle, as parishioners crowded the
Trinity Episcopal Church in Copley Square
and stood about the stone steps, in disbelief,
trying to grasp the unthinkable, death by suicide.
In the public library across the square
old men warmed themselves and slept
at wooden tables in windowless rooms
overlooking the square three stories below.
Office workers hurrying back from lunch
saw the crowds, the mounted police, the church
reflected in the glass of the Prudential Building,
a smaller, darker version marked off in a grid
like art students use to reduce a scene to
manageable proportions, and heard the
congregation singing *Lord Have Mercy*.

The day the bishop was buried,
a couple sat at a small round table, arguing
in different languages, after all those years

unable to make the other understand, unable
to say what they meant, until one of them spoke of
"distance" and "separation," and the other agreed
they were that miserable, the rain dripping off their coats
and into their shoes, their coffee turning cold.
They looked past each other out into the street,
unsure now what to do about all those things
they had planned together for this weekend
or this month or ever. How were they to manage?
Should they separate at once? Should one of them
take the car they'd left at the lot an hour ago
and leave the other to find a different way
home, wherever home might be.

The day the bishop was buried, planes took off
over Boston Harbor, through fog and thick clouds,
carrying passengers into the bright wintry day,
as pink light rippled over an ocean of cloud. Settling
into the dark cabin, lulled by the steady hum, the
rhythmic pulsing through the soles of their feet,
they flew toward afternoon, gaining the hours lost
earlier that week, gazing a long way down
as onto deep fields of snow. If only they knew where to look,
they could perhaps see the remnants of prayer for the bishop
sent up earlier that morning, his footprints leading away
across the clouds. Unless he had stayed behind
in Copley Square and was now slowly
circling the park among the gulls and pigeons,
or standing beneath a black umbrella, or
sitting in silence on a bench, penitent
as his fellow clergy carried the body down
the slick steps and into the waiting hearse.

ONLY THE DISHES

VIRGINIA LEE

Only the dishes remained
A purple insulated tumbler
half-filled with a pinkish mix
of what had been red Gatorade and ice.
Dried up bagel crumbs on a snowman festooned plate
The butter knife next to the sink
with streaks from a sneaky feline tongue.

I stood in the darkened foyer, surrounded by stillness
The signs of life were there, but no voices.
The TV that was her constant background noise dark and silent.
A cleared counter where the two-gallon tank sat
An empty fish-food container, the only sign of what had been.

A white extension cord stretched from outlet to sofa
No longer attached to her computer
seemed forlorn and unwanted.
A maroon plush blanket waited on the chair
Indentations of her body still visible.

The blanket, left for me to keep
a reminder until the next time.
Three weeks - twenty-one days; so much to do together
Winter break goes by too quickly
so many plans unfinished before it's time to go.
Four hours and hundreds of miles separate us
but she is not truly gone
Reminders of her presence are everywhere
clothes, shoes, books
And her dishes, they all remained.

TALKING TO STRANGERS

MARCIE MCGUIRE

Sometimes women I don't know
will stop me—at the checkout,
in the park, on buses,
sometimes in public restrooms,
a woman will grasp my arm
as though she meant
to ask directions
and then forgot
and now stands wondering
how she came to be
clinging to a stranger,
foolishly patting her hand.
She will tell me stories
I never wanted to hear.
Perhaps she will say
I remind her of someone
she used to know,
or she will simply
fix her eyes on me
and ask do I think

people get older in Heaven,
because come Saturday,
she will be sixty,
a year older
than her mother.

THERE IS LOVE ~ ALL AROUND YOU

LISA ADAMS-LLOYD

There is love in the snow
As it dapples the sky
It lands on your head
And your tongue if you try

It falls on your shoulders
Sits perched on your lashes
Sprinkling its kiss
With dropping doled dashes

There is love in the rain
And it sees it way through
To your heart it will carry
Away songs that are blue

Down the road they will travel
Though it might take all day
But don't give up hope
Before you know they're washed away

There is love in the sunshine
No need to ask why
It fills up your spirit
And soul like the sky

Seals the cracks and the creases
And spreads through the air
Lifts the world and diffuses
Flushing wash of your cares

There is love in the wind
Slipping over the catches
It freckles your nose
Welling over in batches

A brush through the willows
And the tall growing grass
Seize the love that you need
For the rest, it will pass

There is love in the clouds
That gently drift through
Distancing the under-song
Of worries undo

There is love in a grove
A forest of trees
That will send your heart soaring
Bringing doubts to their knees

Under the swing of the canopy
You will find what you seek
A smile to your face
Bringing warmth to your cheeks

There is love in the snow
As it falls from the sky
Together we walk
Hand in hand, you and I

IT IS THE END OF A PERFECT DAY

You read to me from your newest copy
of Billy Collins whose poetry we admire.
We found this one in the stacks
at a used book store—Yellow Dog—
as we walked the downtown sidewalks
of Columbia, Missouri.

We ate lunch at El Rancho,
then crossed the street
for sweet fresh cookies hot from the oven—
you chocolate chip, and I red velvet.

And so we minded the traffic lights
and crosswalk signs
not so much to lose weight,
but to return you to health
recently challenged with cancer.
The Columbia Art League gallery
which had a new juried display
prompting discussions of various pieces.

We enjoyed a film at the Ragtag—
Leave no Trace—
of an injured war vet and his teen daughter.
As the film wound to its conclusion,
so did this tiny family's road diverge
amid the brush and forest in life's travel
like a Frost poem.

My eyes scan the edge of your cheek,
and I want more and pray
our road will not split any time soon.

PRIORITIES

NANCY JO ALLEN

The young girl dances with two
white bags in front of the counter:
she is ready to leave. Her father
gathers four large drinks in a tray
balancing four small sundaes atop.

Outside, in the parking lot,
they load the car and it won't start.
It's a large older vehicle without a dealer
or make emblem with little paint,
and no finish.

The man gets out and lifts the hood
performs an act he seems familiar with
under the metal panel. He
directs the young girl to turn the starter
or give it gas. It turns over.

He returns to the cab,
she moves over,
he backs the car out of the stall,
onto the street with shiny mag wheels
to carry them home to the family.

STRATEGIES

NANCY JO ALLEN

I play the Queen of Hearts
on the King of Spades
hoping to free up the Diamond
Ace and start building bottom to top.
As I gaze at the possibilities
in front of me to win at solitaire,
I listen to the comforting hum
of the dishwasher scrubbing residue.
I think of my childhood kitchen
in my leisure after dinner.
My parents cozy on the sofa
together listening to the war coverage
holding on to hope my brothers
will receive *4F* status. My sister
purges dinner into the toilet,
then primps her hair before her date.
One brother watches The Twilight Zone,
two play softball with neighborhood boys
in good health awaiting their fates
with low Selective Service lottery numbers.

DON'T BE SURPRISED

TERRY ALLEN

Don't be surprised. It's not unusual
for your four-year-old to see ghosts.
It's very common here, we were told
by just about everyone we met
including locals and colleagues
when we arrived in Jakarta
after a twenty-four-hour trip
from Chicago to Indonesia.

And once we were in Jakarta,
it was explained that it was important
that we employ as many locals
as possible because we were
wealthy Americans and could hire
a housekeeper or two, a cook,
a gardener, a driver, a babysitter,
and of course, a guard
to keep us safe at home.

Safe? Okay, that's fine,
but what about the ghosts? we asked.
They normally don't hurt people,
we were told, but to be safe
it's best to sleep with the lights on.

But why our four-year-old?
Why would he see ghosts?
Oh, children haven't been here
as long as adults, and are more open
to the trapped souls of the dead.
For them, the veil is thin,
but don't worry, they're rarely harmed;
although, some ghosts are known
to follow them into their dreams.
Besides, children are able to talk
with the spirits more easily than adults,
unless the ghosts don't speak at all.
Like the floaty, white-haired woman
in the long pale dress
who wanders about the house at night.
It's best to stay away from her. She bites.
But not to worry, these wounds
seldom become severely infected
and require amputation.

Still, most of the ghosts
appear to like children,
and they play well together,
but even then, it's wise
to keep in mind the local proverb:
Calm water does not mean
there are no crocodiles.

LAVA PILE

GAIL DENHAM

Choosing a path through dense forest, I
walk toward forever. A wall of stone blocks
the way – lava from an upheaval that shifted
ground as far away as Montana.

Black rock spreads for miles, like fog that
keeps Portland blind during winter months.
Finally I sit on a favorite rock.

A storm blew the chimney off Grandpa Earl's
house one night. Sounded as if the volcano
had belched again. I remember thunder echoed
down the stovepipe; jagged forks of brilliant
storm zigzagged through the kitchen; jolts
rattled Grandma Ida's favorite Dresden doll
figure to the edge of the shelf.

Grandma caught the doll just in time. I could
imagine the enormous blowout from nearby
mountains when they spit hot lava all those

years ago; the explosions moved hills, burned
trees where they stood, caused rivers to boil
and carve new paths.

Fortunate that the lava flow stopped
at the entrance to my woods.

MAJESTY

GAIL DENHAM

Miles and miles of quiet rock walls
and scattered hills line up for inspection
as we drive through Arizona and Nevada.
These ancient uprisings are unaware
of their majestic beauty.

We ask few explanations from these
monuments, some left after surrounding
dried up lakes that once covered this land.
Some have been heaved into place
by volcanoes.

Slowly we pass, often overcome by their
magnificent forms. Other times, as sunset
paints gold on the stones, then green tints
spread, and finally gray shadows cover
all, our chatter ceases.

We revel in the silent brilliance, admire
their enormous strength, knowing they've

endured lightning, torrential rains, flash
floods, heavy snows. Hunters, explorers,
gold miners, pioneers passed here. What tales
these stoic walls could tell.

Antelope, coyotes, badgers, rabbits, snakes,
mountain goats, scorpions, and cougars call
these rocks home. Doubtless Indian tribes lived
among the rock forts, thankful for protective
walls and deep caves.

These roadside sentinels command respect.

MY BEAUTIFUL DAY

...SO GRAND

GAIL DENHAM

"It's late. Evening bells are ringing.
"Best get ourselves away home."
Me best friend, Rosie,
sounds the warning.

We'd joyed all afternoon behind
old Mr. Jacob's place where
a spring bubbled into a small pond.
We'd splashed and laughed
in the clear water for hours.

Now, barefoot and dripping, I run
toward home, pigtails flapping.
Mum would be in a fuss if I was
late to tea. Still, I had to stop and pat
my favorite tree, where green moss
glowed in the fading light.

I skid into the kitchen. Mum pours
out the last cup of tea. To my surprise

she doesn't box me ears as I scoot
into a chair. Perhaps she sees how
the happy lights me face. My favorite
treacle pudding is placed before me.

"Oh I wish you'd been with us, Mum,"
I proclaim between bites of pudding. "I do
wish that. You should have been me."

BEYOND THESE WATERS

KEN GIERKE

Stars open among the lilies.
Are you not blinded by such expressionless sirens?
This is the silence of astounded souls.

Sylvia Plath, Crossing the Water

I look into the depths between the lilies,
beyond the darkness, to see
the light held by the stars reflected there.
There is a sheen in that light dripping
from my fingers as they trail through the water.
A light not so distant, not so silent.
Its voice calls to me, reminds me that
not every siren will lead me to further darkness,
that light can conquer shadow.
I follow that voice to a current of my own making,
away from waters that would stagnate me,
would assign me to a place not meant for me.

From the surface of these waters to the fish at my fingertips,
from the trees on the banks to the land that holds them,
there is not one thing that cannot be brought into this light.
This sign is not a valedictory.
It is a welcoming sight inviting me to be in the light,
astounded by all that I see.

MEASURE OF GRACE

KEN GIERKE

There is a measure of grace
in your layers, kept within
till finally known to the world,

the accelerated tempo
of your cry now in the forefront,
no excuses accepted.

None made.
All sides of this story play
the same. Mothers and daughters

standing beside sisters,
refusing the slow march
of time, refuting submission.

TRUE ENLIGHTENMENT

KEN GIERKE

inspiration found
in deepest depths of darkness
inner light revealed

the one true focus
at the center of being
is found in balance

sincere transcendence
of luminescent being
disperses darkness

true enlightenment
recognizes no center
unless all are one

HOTEI LAUGHING BUDDHA
(IN ISOSYLLABIC 8 FORM)
ANNE GIFFORD

Traditional wood frame houses,
Generations live together.
Fusuma sliders divide rooms,
Rice paper shoji window shades.

Bamboo tatami mat flooring,
Zabuton cushioned mat seating.
Quilt duvet covers Washitsu,
Sunken hearth hibachi heater.

Statue stands on corner altar,
Composed of stone, jade, wood, brass, bronze.
Happy Hotei, Shinto God Man,
Patron saint of all fishermen.

Japanese deity of wealth,
God of contentment and good luck,
God of plentiful and money,
God of blessings and contentment.

Tenth century Japan legend,
Laughing Buddha Hotei-osho.
Protuberant large round belly,
with breasts exposed beneath loose robe.

Symbol of prosperity, luck,
Happiness, fortune, and wisdom.
Ancient chieftain right hand holds fan,
To Represent authority.

Hotei, Wagon Priest sits in cart,
Pulled through city streets to town square.
Contagious laughter fills the air,
Enlightenment and Nirvana.

Carries large bulging linen bag,
Filled with treats and gifts for children.
Eccentric wide grinning kind man,
Like American Santa Claus.

THE HOLIDAY MUM

ANNE GIFFORD

I emerged from the ground of life, nurtured by a horticulturist
Watered and fertilized, pruned of unhealthy tads of suckers
A bright orange ribbon, a Thanksgiving card attached
Placed on a counter and attractively poised in grandeur.

I broke free from the shelf, only to be loaded in a dark trunk
Where is the sun? Where is the water? How will I flourish?
Where are my nursery friends? My succulence is gone. I'm dry
It's lonely in the bleak darkness. Until . . . the trunk opens.

The brilliance of the sun breaks forth amidst the darkness
Beams of light prevail, my leaves absorb the fresh air
Free to bloom forth with golden blossoms and lush foliage
Placed into the hands of the innocent, "Thank you," "Lovely."

Day after day, activity of all ages abounds my subtle presence
Watered and admired, I pose in the presence of the visitors
Thriving with routine watering, I flourish within the warmth
Odiferous aromas of richly seasoned foods fill my surroundings.

Until one day, all is quiet. Outside the window, cold air looms
Flakes of white fall from the sky and clouds hide the sun
Absent is the frivolity of chattering voices as quiet prevails and
I'm embraced in the arms of the one who valued my presence.

I felt loved, until . . . I'm discarded like rubbish into a rusty bin
In the cold, the white flakes of death cover me. Why? I ask.
Why not preserve my existence and bury me in the flowerbed?
Then, come next fall, I could return to bloom forth once again.

BREAD IS POETRY

MELINDA HEMMELGARN

If you follow your nose
down a quiet tree-lined street
tucked into the heart of the city
you'll find a welcoming
red-brick house.

Stay on the scent
down the pebble path,
unlock the gate, and there,
the brick oven stands
birthing loaves of sacred bread
warm and golden, they
have risen to the occasion
of nourishing a community.

Neighbors greet and taste
shower praise on the baker
and wrap their precious loaves
gently in cloth, to make their journey home.

On warm evenings, wine
joins the bread, with laughter
and conversation
and for a little while
the world is at peace
we feel connected, held in time
by flour, yeast, water and salt
bread, hands, heart.

SAYING GOODBYE

MELINDA HEMMELGARN

It's hard to know when, exactly
it'll be that one last time
to hold a grandchild
embrace a sibling
kiss a lover
or hug a friend.

Death may come suddenly
like a head on collision
or it may invade slowly,
like a cancer, creeping
one cell at a time
before taking its final grasp.

So celebrate each day
savor its rhythms
take note and listen
to all our connections -
the birdsong at daybreak
crickets at night.

Observe the silvery dew drops
inhale the aroma of rain
feel the sun soak into your skin
dwell on the sweetness of life
look up at the glimmering stars
deep in the vast open sky.

Rejoice, in the exuberance of spring
the eternal cycles of life.
Find beauty
in the ever so small
in the miracles around us
we're part of them all.

AFTER THE STORM

ON CAPE SAN BLAS

MARY HORNER

I saw the past
Hanging like strings
From the rafters.

The temptation to pull
One might bring down
The entire house.

The beauty of destruction
Might have gone unnoticed
Like the breeze.

Because I always want to go
Home, regardless of
The consequences.

ANSWERS

MARY HORNER

Time drew a conclusion on
Her face she knew nothing about,
So, she filled in some
Of the blank spaces with
A foundation of lies and deceit,
(A luxury she could not afford)
Which were highlighted
When she stepped outdoors,
All unbeknownst to her
And the beauty influencer.

FOLLOW THE DAY

MARY HORNER

The early sun lifts culture into place
Trapped by illogical logic, but
Accepted nonetheless for hours
That hold us hostage to our beliefs and daylight.

Replaced by a moon that opens the
Door to romance hiding secrets behind the
Shadows, careful not to
Bring them out too early.

Rolling hills of sleep
Turn thoughts into music we compose
And flags into kites
That disappear into a yellow sky.

Dusk is where we breathe a space
Between two worlds that doesn't
Distinguish our beliefs, so examine
The day closely through a dark lens.

Remove it at night, when
magic releases the chains and we
See each other for who we are,
And ourselves.

AWAKENING: A HAIKU

WANITA MARIE HUMPHREY

Sounds slowly seep in,
Eyelids begin to flutter,
My world comes alive.

WORLD PEACE?

WANITA MARIE HUMPHREY

A world in miniature, I take my place
Amid a table and chairs with bright cushions.
Before me, a tableau, framed:
Horizontal borders--the porch floor and ceiling,
Verticals, the roof's supporting posts.
The setting, a rectangle of grass, the backdrop—red cedar, hickory and
Two varieties of oak.
A double shepherd's hook offers two feeders,
Seeds for small birds and the fat black sunflower seeds
Coveted by larger feathered and fur baring creatures.
Trilling notes announce first arrival, on a bare branch,
Bright red, peaked head, proud stance, haughty glance,
The cardinal boasts, "I have a place! Lady, come share!"
Squirrels stretch, back feet on tree, front feet holding
The cage of treats. Stretching, rocking, nibbling.
Precarious position loosens an unchewed shower
To the ground below to those who await the falling bounty.
Jays, usual tattle-tales, quietly share with a dove, mechanically
Bobbing her head to the feast. Small birds have also dropped
Morsels being retrieved by fellows below.

A chipmunk weaves its way among thin legs with no
Fuss or bother. No barking from the squirrels as a bird
Lands on the same feeder. Titmouse, finch, and downy—
Or hairy? I can never remember which, but the red head is there.
A delicate huff. I freeze in my shadow-box behind the frame.
The doe with the twin fawns emerges from the trees.
She is cautious—I am still—she allows the babies to
Advance.
In this world of diverse creatures, there is no strife, no
Division, no hate—only peace and sharing.
Only one element has the power to disturb the tranquility
—the human element.
—I do not move.
—I respectfully observe the respectful interaction and think,
"If only…if only…."

THE RIGHT THANK YOU

MARILYN HOPE LAKE

The goldfinch was released today;
left my nested hands
without a thank you.

When first taken in,
it's dark wing
with bright white bars,
lay limp,
too injured to fly.

Today,
it flew like a bullet
into the sky.

I spied the goldfinch this morn,
out on the drive,
midst other backyard birds,
feasting on sunflower and
nyler seed.
All the thanks I'll ever need.

CONCATENATION

LYNNE JENSEN LAMPE

Black fur puddled at the bottom
of a shelter cage, you slowly stretch
a front leg through bars, swat air
when you hear my voice.
Magnanimous, you retract your claws,
let me capture your paw. My finger
traces a whorl of fur. I wait for the rumble,
the purr. Your tongue slips out, a tiny
tab of pink contentment.

*

You, whose kin ruled with Cleopatra,
deign to be crated as baggage
during travel, your lithe body spiraled
like a mountain mahogany seed, energy
building until we reach home. You unfurl
and leap in our apartment off Broadway,
flaunt your haunches in the street-level
window, accept praise from passersby

heading to coffee or the clubs.

*

Slinking through tall grass and conduit,
you slay rodent, snake, illness,
insecurity before they can devour me.
Agile as new love, your plump velvet feet
pad along the rim of the clawfoot tub
while I bathe. You join my evening rambles,
snuggle beneath my covers as I sleep.

*

Nineteen years of light
dwindle to a day
expected yet unbid.
Your stare commands
me to hasten the end.
Your ragged
paw traces my jaw.

EMILY CARR PAINTS ANOTHER FOREST INTERIOR

LYNNE JENSEN LAMPE

In the belly of the forest, silence
feeds the golden hour
to Douglas firs and mountain
hemlock, an afternoon swell

of light. Your feet are not the first
to travel the waist of these hills
but you, crone, paint as if.
As if you have a lover

and trees seek your sap.
As if what you grind
into house paint and gasoline
will create life on the page,

the only kind of reproduction
you and I will know.
The irony of paper wearing
pigment in tribute

to its source,
yet less than—three dimensions
made two. Fine-boned
saplings rib the hillside,

yearn for your fat
strokes of green and blue.
In time you'll marry
earth, but today breathe

wave after waterless wave.
Orange, umber, black
silence hums the forest
floor. Autumn air begs

the question lovers never ask:
How many suns
can you hold
before starting to burn?

SALT GROWS NOTHING

LYNNE JENSEN LAMPE

When the men beat fists on our door
& lay claim to our guests,
my husband sought to sacrifice
two of our daughters. *Virgins*
he yelled, an auctioneer
with sheer tissue to unload.
I hated him again

for piercing my body
with his own
on our wedding night,
planting his flag of seeds
in a fertile land that belonged
only to me. My body
poured salt & iron
& he called me dirty

until the day he thought
his seed had grown a boy.
But no. My always-wound

cleaned itself of four girls
in as many years. I scattered
each with salt to comfort them
after the ocean of my womb,
to harden them to the rites
of men, the fathers & sons
who think clouds own the rain.

Lot claimed our children
were his to gamble.
I wanted to take the girls
& leave & never look back.
But two stayed in town
to take care of their men.
Thunder & salt poured
from my throat, my fists.
The guests—angels—flung
loaves & wineskins at us,
hustled us out before God
destroyed all hope.

Those men who wrote
the Book got me wrong.
My name isn't Wife.
I didn't spurn heaven.

PROMISE ME

STEPHANIE LANGAKER

Promise me
as you hold me
against your chest,
calming me with your voice,
allowing your steady heartbeat
to take on and reset my racing one;
As you allow the flood of
worries to pour, with the words from my mouth
and the tears from my eyes,
all the while remaining
not unmoved,
but steady,
full of love and patience and strength;

Promise me
you will let me hold you
in my arms,
reassuring you with my voice,
allowing my gentle hands
to remove your shame and self-doubt;

That you will allow the darkness of
despair to cover us both for a spell,
all the while knowing
that I remain
not unmoved,
but steady,
full of love and patience and strength.

THAT WHICH BELONGS TO ME

STEPHANIE LANGAKER

I cannot possess your heart
Any more than I can possess the sea.

For when I am in or on the waves of the sea,
I am at its mercy
and can be euphoric or frightened or disoriented.

But when I am not there,
The sea continues to be pulled through its tides,
And I cannot control who else may be at its mercy.

I cannot possess your heart
Any more than I can possess a river.

For when I stand by a river,
I cannot fathom its depth,
Nor do I know all that it brings from upstream.

A river may change its course,
So one must accept that dwelling near it

And depending upon it
May last a lifetime;
Or may end suddenly in a flood;
Or may just disappear over time
so gradually that,
by the time you realize what is happening,
It is too late.

But I can own my questions
And when I am satisfied with the answers.

I can own my time
And decide when it is worth spending.

I can own the real estate
Upon which my house of dreams is built
And torn down
And built again.

AN OUTSIDER

VIRGINIA LEE

Suitcases trailing behind them
Arms full of treasures that needed to be held
My daughters walk to the front door of their dad's house.
It used to be my house too, until decisions were made
decisions with consequences for many people.

They want me to come in
I hesitate, wondering how much longer I will be allowed inside.
The house is now occupied by a new fiancé and her children
My girls the only connection I have to this house.

I am the outsider now, the one who doesn't belong.

The house holds memories
which can be re-lived when I step inside
even if I was the one to cause all of this.
Every room brings a memory, some brighter than others.

The screened-in porch, a favorite gathering spot
a place of tea parties, birthday parties and cuddling;

The backyard koi pond, a peaceful oasis created by us
a place to sit, watch the fish
and the sun reflect in the waterfall.
A backyard where pets were buried
and two weeping willows were planted
in memory of lost children.
Deep in the backyard
An in-ground fire-pit crafted by their father and me
where the deer wore trails into the grasses.

A place that had gone from a house to a home
And now, to me, it would be just a house once more
An outsider looking in.

LEMON SNAPS

VIRGINIA LEE

Below the ladder
Where the divers enter
the ocean bubbles and churns.

A multitude of dorsal fins slice the surface
Yellowish-brown speckled bodies
turning and twisting, darting and diving.
Always together, social sharks with a hierarchy
each knows their place.

Eyes roll back, protective membrane covering them.
Motion quick and snake-like
Sharp teeth flashing, jaws snapping
but never making contact.

The sharks know the signal – a silenced engine equals food.
These bottom dwellers rise to the surface
Anticipating the splash
Chum, frozen fish popsicles – fishsicles – delicious snacks
Are why the lemon sharks snap.

I FEEL WEEPY TODAY

BARBARA LEONHARD

At long last, it is raining,
though we were hoping for snow.
Christmas has passed
into a drive by the river.

The fields are plowed,
but the seeds must wait, as I do,
for a better year.

Congregations of red-winged blackbirds
populate the trees like leaves.
As I pass, the birds scatter,
lifting up as one song,
the flock casting
into a murmuration,
a dancing swell of a black billow
over the upturned earth.

The birds descend like raindrops,
clustering into a wave

that drifts to a crest,
then collapses into a swirl
that dances across the field
in a ballet for late day sun.

Above them circles a red-tailed hawk
tracking its prey,
and I am mesmerized
into tears.

IT'S ALL ABOUT DEATH, REALLY

BARBARA LEONHARD

The gap between compassion and surrender is love's darkest, deepest region.

— ORHAN PAMUK, THE MUSEUM OF INNOCENCE

I am ready to shed the old clothes,
the tatters that hang off my heart that I thought
held some comfort but that no longer fit me.
I lay them out for display. Touch each one,
each fear and attachment one last time.

I release my hoard of wants and needs.
My weight I put on for protection. My addictions
to coffee, chocolate, red wine.
My attraction to numbing routines,
like scrolling my way through the 'daze' as though
my time has passed.

I let go of unhealthy relationships. Minds that no longer
hold resonance to mine, may you be well.
I'll miss you, but I no longer grieve your absence
or fear abandonment.
I forgive you and myself.
I'm moving on into my vast true nature,
which holds inner wisdom and guidance
from my own tribe. I know my soul mates
will never retire.

I unburden myself from other worries. Fear of illness
and joint failure. Fear of falling.
Fear of success. Fear of defeat.
Fear of being a woman in a misogynistic world.
Fear of love and intimacy. Fear of crowds.
Fear of judgment and ridicule.
Fear of losing my mind to social dementia.

I disengage my rationalizations and projections.
They have only misled me into thinking
that I am not responsible for my pain.
Fear makes me a martyr,
felled by false beliefs.

I surrender my need to be right in any fight.
I can refract and reflect. I can move
in many directions. Not just as rays
but also waves.
Just as Soul.

I relinquish my disdain for my pesky shadow
as I know she is here to teach me,
to terrorize my naked heart
until it screams open,
and I am finally able to see

that I do not need to be 'fixed'.

My soul is no longer broken;
it's outgrown its fears.
Cleansed and ready.
Ready. For what's next.

THE SHAPE OF BREATH

BARBARA LEONHARD

Champagne bubbles billow from the big bang.
Spindrift the falling apple toward glasses
raised in "Auld Lang Syne". The bubbles rise,

some glorious, some clinging to others,
some wet drizzle. They snap and burst into bated breath.
Tickle the once free-spirited. Today

we're locked down by confining capsids.
Our colors bend around frowns.
Dampen the confetti. We're as novel

as the boy in the plastic bubble[1]. The one
who couldn't breathe our diseased air
taught us how to survive. To leave fingerprints

on the inside, not the outside. The danger
of poking holes in the bubble. The way to entrap
the nose inside a bulbous helmet to prevent infection

outside the bubble. The tug of the umbilical cord
when we venture out to view the eclipse. The loneliness
of reaching for gloved hands offering toys.

But haven't the presidents, the royals, and billionaires
always chosen the air they breathe
in their privileged pied-à-terre?

Even the monks, though loving all kind,
sequester in rising sun. Their prayers
spark, pop, dissolve in the mountain air.

Community - an illusion? Our bubbles orbit each other.
We get to survive – yet forget the scent of skin,
the warmth of an embrace, the pressure of soft lips.

Our faces stare back at us in the shimmer of wet breath.
We burst from the same source but find our joy trapped
as spherical oscillating floating things,

    bouncing off others,
    spiraling into fog.

---

1.   https://www.cbsnews.com/pictures/bubble-boy-40-years-later-look-back-at-heartbreaking-case/

SEMOLINA SUNDAYS

FRANK MONTAGNINO

My family looks forward to Sunday.
That's the day we have a big meal.
On Sunday we always eat pasta.
We think pasta's a very big deal.

Some folks may feel it's boring,
Eating pasta one day every seven.
But pasta, I say, is what they eat every day
In Italy and, I'll wager, in Heaven.

Yep. Pasta every Sunday. At my house we just love it.
And because it's so very versatile, we never tire of it.

There's spaghetti, of course, the old pasta mainstay.
And little brother spaghettini;
You cook them both the same way.

Boil the pasta 'til 'al dente.' (Just right to the tooth.)
You'll love it covered with meat sauce.
And that, is the God's honest truth.

Bucatini however, is sturdier. It's stiff enough to fight back.
It throws tomato sauce everywhere, unless you have a knack
For twirling your pasta neatly up on your fork
To get rid of long strands that make you look like a dork,

Dangling out of your mouth and down on your chin
Then retracting juicily when you suck them all in.

LaSagna's a whole different kettle of fish.
It's a wide, ribboned noodle you bake in a dish.
It's layered with meat sauce and ricotta cheese,
Then baked in the oven. This one's sure to please.

Then there's Pasta Fagioli. (Some say "Pasta Fazool.")
White beans with pasta. Comfort food that's old school.

A plateful of linguini with fresh, tender clams.
Is great for your taste buds if not your cardiograms.

Another great pasta we can't oversell
Is a wide, flat noodle that's called tagliatelle.
Sometimes this fine pasta comes coiled in a nest.
And with Bolognese sauce, oh my word, it's the best.

Of course, there's always tortellini, or capellini or ditallini.
And Alfredo's famous fettuccini.
Fettuccini Alfredo blends thick, rich cream
With parmigiano reggiano. And it's fit for a queen.

Ravioli, cannelloni, mostaccioli, rigatoni, macaroni….
There's even one called campanelle. It's shaped like a bell,
And it goes very well, with a nice zinfandel.

There. Seventeen pastas. And there are lots more than these,
So, one every Sunday fills me with -
Calories.

CHANGE WITH THE SEASONS

DEBBIE PARKER

Vernal Equinox brings wonder, beauty, new life.
Pups, kits, owlets, fawns, eaglets
Roam, play and learn life's rules.
Rebirth for predator and prey.
Snowdrops burst through the crusted earth
Towards the longer days of light.
Verdant fields of jewelweed, rose turtlehead,
Sky blue aster and Indian grass wave to one another.
Orange and black monarchs reign on goldenrod stalks
Return the wave of the bloomers.

Autumnal Equinox makes itself known with strong gusts
Denuding trees that leave bare arms reaching for the sun.
Squirrels bury caramel nuts in crisp, scarlet,
Vermillion and burnt umber maple leaves.
Geese honk a greeting as they soar overhead
While indigo buntings look for a warmer clime.
Deer graze among the sea oats, golden coreopsis
Joe Pye, sneezeweed, and Indian paintbrush.

Both seasons have equal parts turbulence and beauty.
Human life being part of nature,
Tries to grow, adapt and change
With each yearly trip around the Sun.

THE GOSSIP

DEBBIE PARKER

The gossip heats her cauldron using the sticks and stones
Once thrown at the ones she perceived as weak.
She dips her prey into the boiling stew of lies,
And twists and turns the truth to make
something totally unrecognizable.

The gossip covers her victims with sticky rumors
Impossible to remove and tosses them aside to rot.
Then she moves on to the next unsuspecting victim
who believes her when she shares
information they need to know

THUNDERSTORM HARMONY

Tranquil bed. Peaceful sleep.
Small body clamors onto me.
Nose to nose she stares.
Whimpers, "Grandma."

"Scared?" I ask.
Frantic shake of curls.
Lightning flash. Thunder boom.
I lift the quilt. She scurries in.

Quick footsteps.
Here comes big sister.
Quivering voice, "I'm scared, too."
Sweet, sweaty snuggles.

Quiet. I doze.
Thunder rumbles.
Wiggle, squirm, whimper.
Gentle caresses.

Water patters on window.
"Can I take you to your room?"
Heads shake, No!
Burrow into Grandma.

Arm around each,
Deep breath,
I tell myself. S*tay still.*
Sleep in this crowded bed.

I patiently wait.
Girls motionless.
Rhythmic breathing.
Carefully, I rise.

Eyes snap open.
Tenderly stroke head.
"You two stay in my bed."
Sisters snuggle.

Soft guest bed.
Peaceful room.
Distant rumble.
Sleep.
…Sleep.
……Sleep

Scent of pancakes on griddle.
Grandpa clatters dishes.
Little girl voices.
"Where's Grandma?"

"Here I am. Sleep well?"
Girls nod and smile.
"That was quite the storm."
Grandpa turns, "What storm?"

BEAUTY, CREATED

MARY CAITLYN RODRIGUEZ

I saw love.
Wounds and stitches,
Scars –
Beauty.
They moved in unison pouring sand into a glass jar,
Layer by layer, dark mixed with light.
No pattern or intention,
Just graceful movements,
Guessing –
Beauty.

I watched the process unfold,
Unblinking and captivated.
They looked to each other
And I saw hope,
As if the sand held their dreams.
I wanted to scream for intentionality,
To be able to mold the sand as it slides off hands,
A plan –
On purpose beauty.

But they kept looking to each other,
Guiding, guessing together –
Beauty.
The jar filled to the brim,
No pattern or intention,
Morphed into a design.
Beauty that wouldn't be possible
Without dark and light mixed together
Seamlessly for a purpose –
Beauty.

They turned towards each other,
Eyes danced with newness,
In beginnings.
And I couldn't help but wonder,
What if the jar broke?
Impossible to clean up every grain,
Pointless to scoop handfuls
With no jar to pour into.
Broken –
Beauty?

Everything looks the same when it is broken,
Nothing looks the same when pieced back together.
Rough edges, cracked uniquely;
Layers of darkness covered by light.
A new shade created –
Beauty.

FRIEND UNTIL BETRAYED

MARGARET SETTLE

Hello from afar
Hello old friend
Friend reminiscing
Friend reconnecting
Reconnecting old times
Reconnecting memories
Memories we shared
Memories we cherished
Cherished a friendship
Cherished adventures
Adventures and journeys
Adventures that changed
Changed a perspective
Changed a view
View of a friend
View from a distance
Distance needed
Distance took
Took what wasn't hers
Took him away

Away from a home
Away from a future
Future without him
Future stolen
Stolen heart
Stolen dreams
Dreams of a family
Dreams of perfection
Perfection or fantasy
Perfection flawed
Flawed friendship
Flawed friend
Friend or foe
Friend and truth
Truth is painful
Truth reveals
Reveals a cheat
Reveals the dishonest
Dishonest words
Dishonest trust
Trust shattered
Trust destroyed
Destroyed marriage
Destroyed friendship
Friendship gone
Friendship betrayed
Betrayed forever
Betrayed and lost
Lost
Forever

LEAFY WORKERS

SUSETTE V. SHREVE

Early spring brings life to the forest's factories.
Dressed in shades of green each worker
Responsible for his product. From sun-up
To sun-down CO2 in, O2 out! Daylight
Filters gently through a canopy of leaves.
Winds shift leafy branches making tree limbs
Dance from side to side, up to down.
Musical beats are tapped out first high then
Low, soft then loud with a final flutter to
Stillness. A feast to the ears or a warning
Of danger? Eventually days grow short, production
Dwindles. Green uniforms are replaced with jazzy
Reds, golds, oranges, and browns. Workers are
Let go, drifting without purpose. It is now
Time to reinvent.

THERE UPON LOVED

SUSETTE V SHREVE

Sail a boat
Sail here or there
There to go
There to where
Where I'll be
Where there's love
Love so splendor
Love of passion
Passion played out
Passion past
Past as present
Past with memories
Memories so cherished
Memories faded
Faded slow
Faded fast
Fast as seconds
Fast years fly
Fly out the window
Fly passed the sun

Sun shining bright
Sun setting too soon
Soon I'll go
Soon to find
Find anew
Find another
Another one
Another two
Two of a pair
Two of a kind
Kind to each other
Kind of nice
Nice to see
Nice to wonder
Wonder what
Wonder how
How the future
How it holds
Holds the present
Holds what's passed
Passed with sugar
Passed with spice
Spice enhanced
Spice of life
Life well lived
Life well loved
Loved forever
Loved so cherished
Cherished
Forever

ONE MAN'S TRASH

SHARON SINGINGMOON

1
A connoisseur of that which is no longer useful
Charlie's sport is privy digging
the dust, detritus
dregs of forgotten families
pottery shards & bits of china
doll's heads, maybe an antique watch
crusted with ancient night soil
composted into the fine and fertile

He flaunts his rebel nature
shakes a trowel as archeologists cringe
there is potential in garbology
money to be made in the pontiled
medicine bottles, ink containers -
collectors clamor for these kick-backs
throw-ins of early life

2

Plat maps in hand, a call is made
diggers arrive in early September
"Opportunistic looters", accuses the curious mayor
of a town now barely there

Just two feet down
already with a trove of pontiled bottles
shovels too heavy for delicate work
the diggers took to trowels
knee-deep in the hole
Charlie's probe sings with expectation
he kneels, gently shifts soft soil
grins, another two feet down and the loot piles up
the property owners shake their heads in wonder

Chest-deep, the man in the hole
examines the side walls for flaking
fearing a collapse will threaten the work
refusing to quit, he kneels
runs a gloved hand across the floor of the hole
brushes away loose soil
reveals a rounded object, too large to be a bottle
pulls a human skull from beneath his left knee

"Hey Joe," he hollers to his partner
"call the cops, we got a skull."
Within an hour, three more skulls and associated bones
lay across the piles of dirt
a local sheriff, two adjunct professors and the mayor
of the town now barely there
stand hands in their pockets

The sheriff moves forward
watches with a sour look as the gloved professors
gently wrap the bones in canvas
load them in a van headed to a lab somewhere
the diggers with a mighty tale to tell
retire to the local pub
their share of the loot forgotten for a time

THE THEORY OF EVERYTHING

SHARON SINGINGMOON

A lack of empirical evidence shall not deter us
nor alternative theories darken the pathway to unification
it is fundamental
gravitons
electrons
photons
the blue stem grass on the prairie, dry seeds blowing in the breeze
the sheets flapping on your Na-Na's clothesline
that insect buzzing in your ear
the mud squeezing up between your toes and you and your ear
and your toes

Absolutely everything

We are all vibrating ribbons of energy
constructed of imperceptibly tiny ribbons of quivering energy
each vibrational pattern distinct, unique

The Mother
M-theory
the theory of everything

Yet, "questions remain," said Simmons-Duffin
and Maldacena, cited in over 16,000 papers over twenty years,
posited particles moving around space-time geometries
infused with negative energy
making them bend in ways different from our universe – black holes
a conformal field

(I, on the other hand, posit a field of wild flowers
stretching across the valley between twin mountain peaks at an altitude
such as to make one dizzy with even just a single glass of chardonnay.

I posit that by lying on one's back quietly,
watching a cumulus parade float across the azure
one may find that deep vibration belonging exclusively to the self
that is lying and gazing, quiet but for the wandering insect buzzing at a
vibratory rate singularly its own.)

It is mathematics, they say
a basic sequence of events, a demonstration of consistency
graviton-graviton scatter calculation
the inability to complete even a first quantum correction
proof enough, some say

M-theory
the Mother

I say
In the forest I understand.

in the mountains, along the shore, when a storm blows through,
as the moon rises, or a baby smiles,
I understand basic math. $1 + 1 = 10{,}000$ billion = One
I understand in ways my simple use of syllables cannot contain

> *In 1995, physicist Edward Witten developed what is known as the Theory of Everything or the Mother Theory (M-Theory). M-theory unifies in a single mathematical structure all five consistent versions of string theory (as well as a particle description called supergravity)*

THE THIEF A VILLAIN – L(OVE)

SHARON SINGINGMOON

there is no harsher sadness than to love a thief
he may come by day, steal your heart that night
he offers just pale shadows of true relief

a romp, a dance, a trusted moment of belief
he smothers you, envelopes you, holds on tight
there is no harsher sadness than to love a thief

times of joy turn bitter when you love a thief
as dark descends, you seek the light
he offers just pale shadows of true relief

you rush to the horizon, chase elusive relief
as you feel his push, taste the bitterness of his spite
there is no harsher sadness than to love a thief

the secrets that you share mean little to a thief
he begs for your attention, even acts contrite
he offers just pale shadows of true relief

he'll hide behind your longing, play upon your grief
he offers just pale shadows of true relief
but cast no blame at your door for you have seen the light
there is no harsher sadness than to love a thief

ESCAPING REALITY

BILLIE HOLLADAY SKELLEY

quickly
open the cover, turn the pages
eyes glued to the twisty black letters
weaving strong, steely bars of protection

slowly
linger over the words, hear the voices
see the faces, feel what they feel
immerse in a world of laughter and love

eventually
there will be no more, the end always comes
covers must be closed, lids must be shut
the tangible world comes back into focus

instantly
yelling, curses slicing through the air
blows raining down, bruises rising up
he perceives weakness, but I'm not weak

for now
I have courage, real strength
enough to leave my refuge, to come back, to fight
but one day, I may surrender

forever
electing to stay safely sheltered between the pages

POISONED

BILLIE HOLLADAY SKELLEY

Your words claim the trouble was all for naught,
stressing we must get back together to heal.

My heart takes flight, dancing at the thought,
but my wounded spirit refuses to kneel.

So foolish the heart, desiring to be caught—
much wiser the soul, tasting the agony still.

TRANSITORY NATURE

BILLIE HOLLADAY SKELLEY

flowers bloom into existence
but petals wither in the cold

fires blaze brightly
but flames die in the ashes

ideas grow in books
but pages turn to dust

lovers grasp at moments
but time slips through their fingers

youth shimmers with promise
but age darkens with regret

reality offers temporary mirages and illusions
but people seek permanence in these fleeting things

FICTION

Photo Credit: Lisa Adams-Lloyd

FICTION JUDGE

Gregory Ashe

Gregory Ashe is a longtime Midwesterner. He has lived in Chicago, Bloomington (IN), and Saint Louis, his current home. He primarily writes contemporary mysteries, with forays into romance, fantasy, and horror. Predominantly, his stories feature LGBTQ protagonists. When not reading and writing, he is an educator.

For more information, visit his website: www.gregoryashe.com.

PLAY FOR ME

MARY HORNER

Miss Genevieve gave my children their piano lessons at her house last week on Tuesday instead of Monday. She usually comes to our house, but the family room and front hall had been painted a bad salmon color and the fumes were still strong on Monday evening. She agreed to lessons at her house the following day.

We pulled to the curb as the rain increased its intensity, and filed up the sidewalk at exactly 4:00 p.m. The piano music seeped out onto the porch, and I would have liked to stay quiet and listen to her play, but one of the kids rang the bell.

"Who's first?" Miss Genevieve asked as we entered.

Hilary walked to the piano just like she did at the recital, with feet made of lead. Fortunately, she had finished her Music Theory lesson minutes earlier in the van. Stephen and I sat down on the beige couch together. He leaned against me while he played his computer game and I began to read a book of sad stories by a French author. After a few minutes Stephen moved to the heating vent on the floor and leaned his back against the pale gray wall.

Through the sheer curtain I could see her front yard, the street and the house of a friend just beyond. In her garden, lights were still attached to the branches of a small tree next to the house. Cold March raindrops raced down the glass as I watched a few cars hurry past on their way home from work, each traveling from left to right through the window frame. I wondered if French rainstorms felt as dreary.

My right hand rested on the arm of the sofa, lifeless as a statue. At one point during the first lesson, my thumb twitched slightly and jerked away from the rest of the hand. A vein on the back of my hand moved just a bit. I stared at it for a few moments to see if it would happen again, but it didn't. It was like watching a frog near the pond. You don't really know if it's going to jump, so you wait for it, but when it happens, it startles you. While I stared, I tried to imagine that I had all my fingers again.

I gave up playing the piano a long time ago. My hand was in constant pain for several months, although it lessened substantially after the first couple of weeks. Phantom pains return occasionally, usually at night in bed before I fall asleep. That's when I wonder where it is, the missing part of me. I picture it living in a lab somewhere with other fingers, being studied for advances in hand surgery, or joint problems, or any other hand maladies that may exist. I'm not sure why I think it would be "living" anywhere.

I still type, though. And I'm good. When I see my hands in the light from the computer screen in a dark room, I notice how rough and full of veins and life and usefulness they are. Sometimes in the day they look beautiful and smooth, but at night they are thick and ugly with twisted veins running through the backs of my hands like vines in the jungle. The skin on my knuckles is wrinkled and stretched beyond imagination over arthritic joints that cry out in pain on rainy mornings.

I like to watch my fingers press the keys. My wrists don't move much, but the fingers reach and strike the various keys in an odd rhythmic pattern. My daughter wanders in occasionally and likes to watch them, too. One hand is beautiful, the other is amazing.

Words flow quickly across the computer screen, as if my fingers are my brain. They glide easily across the keys, so unless you really looked, you wouldn't notice there are only three fingers connected to a palm that comes to an end much too quickly.

"Uneven," some would say, or "Something missing." Most people never notice, and I don't draw attention to it unless I want to, usually when I'm feeling lonely or disconnected, like my pinkie.

Miss Genevieve was too polite to bring up resuming lessons. She is a prominent member of her church, as well as the organist and a good person who would only want to do the right thing. She would probably pray about it, and come up with a way to make things right. But I would feel bad, because there is no solution. Sometimes I want to tell her about the pain, the surgery and the profound fear of dogs. I want to watch her face, and pretend not to be affected by it. Just as a matter of fact, tell her what really happened. But I don't.

Within a few days of my phone call, she had added my children to her roster of students even though her usual waiting list was several months long. They took my old spot. The one I always had on Mondays afternoons at 4:00. My last lesson had been decades earlier in May. School had just let out, and I was looking forward to a lazy summer. We had plans to visit my aunt in Florida.

On the way to her house, I saw Buster, her neighbor's dog, in the yard. Miss Genevieve had told us not to pet him. He was old and crabby, and he didn't like children. She thought he would surely be dead by the time he turned 15, but he hung on. Usually he was put away behind the chain link fence, but I saw her son, Gary, let him out.

Gary was 14, and a target for the bullies on the bus. He was small for his age, wore dark-rimmed glasses and carried a saxophone to school in a black leather case. At home, his little sister took advantage of the fact that she was a tiny blond who could play piano by ear.

"Gary Anderson," I yelled from the yard. "You better put that dog back before his owners find out you opened the gate."

"Oh shut up, you ol' goody two shoes. Mind your own business."

"I'm gonna tell your mama if you don't put that old dog back where he belongs," I said.

"You better not snitch on me, or you'll be sorry."

"No, you'll be sorry if you don't put him back," I said.

"I'm warning you to mind your own business," he said, as he pointed at me. "I'm warning you."

The back of the piano faced the window, so when I sat at the bench I could see outside through the sheers. During the lesson, Gary paced back and forth several times. Sometimes he just pointed his finger at me. Sometimes he scrunched up his face and mouthed the words "I'm warning you." His mother saw none of this.

When I left through the front door, Gary was gone. I could hear Miss Genevieve play a Mozart Concerto from the front porch while she waited for her next student. I don't know how I knew that it was Mozart, but I did. Buster walked toward the house. I thought he was being friendly, so I smiled and said hello to him. I held out my hand to pet him.

I could hear Mozart on the porch. Miss Genevieve was just a couple feet away from me, but she couldn't hear me. Buster leaped toward me, and I screamed. I had never seen him move like that.

He was slow enough that I was able to get out of the way, but since I moved away from the doorbell, there was no way she could hear me as I ran from the house. I dropped my music books and headed toward the street. Buster followed.

Her neighbor said later that he thought I might be able to outrun him, but Buster got his speed and determination from the same place. A dark place deep inside that some might call instinct, and some might call just being a dog. He could still turn it on when he wanted to. Once he began the chase, he wasn't about to let up.

He came closer. I continued down the street, and cried for help. I wanted someone to pick me up. I wanted someone to take me away from the moment. Miss Genevieve's neighbor down the street heard me scream and came outside. I saw him I and thought I was safe. But he turned around. In a split second he ran back into the house.

"Help," I cried, as I watched his door shut behind him.

I looked back. The door opened. He raised a gun in my direction. I dropped to the ground and rolled in the grass. Buster was on me in a second. I covered my head with my hands. He grabbed my right hand in his mouth.

I couldn't see it, but felt saliva and old teeth as they pressed down like a car door right before it slams shut. The smell of adrenalin and old dog surrounded me, and for a moment I thought he was done. But a second later those teeth tore through my skin and mixed with my blood. He fell dead after I heard the bullet explode from the end of the gun.

The blood from my hand dripped in my eyes, and I smeared it trying to wipe it away. Miss Genevieve's neighbor looked horrified as he came toward me. He thought the blood was from my head.

"Who's your kin?" he yelled.

"Walters," I said, weakly. "Past the creek." I tried to point with my left hand.

He ran back into the house to call my parents as I laid in the grass near the sidewalk in front of his house. I couldn't look at my hand, so I looked at the dog. Buster was about a foot away, lying in his own blood. Half his head was gone. I could see one eyeball too close to where his mouth was. It didn't look right.

The neighbor came out and wrapped my mangled hand in a blue towel. He picked up my music and brought it to me. I knew the pages wouldn't be in the right order, but don't know why I cared. Then I heard Mozart again, even though Miss Genevieve had come out onto the porch. I began to cry when I saw my mother's car pull into the driveway.

When the children finished the lessons, we walked through the cold wet grass to the van. Hillary and Stephen climbed in from the side that faced the curb, and then I ran around to get into the driver's seat. A childhood friend yelled a greeting from her house across the street, so I waved and drove off into another week of begging the children to play for me.

MY SON

JANA STEPHANS

For years, life had been nothing but work and worry. In May of 1947, my luck changed. I would be in a position to bring my son home. I drove my dad's 1936 Chevy over to the next small town in rural southern Missouri to give the joyous news to Mrs. Gray, my former mother-in-law. Upon my arrival, Mrs. Gray greeted me with her gracious smile.

"Sit down, Ellen, I'll bring coffee," making me feel like a grand lady being waited on. "I'll go fetch Ronald," she added, leaving the room.

Waiting for my son to appear, I admired Mrs. Gray's elegant living room. Heavy mahogany furniture held lamps and curios, and snowy crocheted antimacassars protected every upholstered piece. Someday I would have a house as splendid, with the perfect living room, just like hers, flawless, but for a fly buzzing behind the closed red brocade draperies. Mrs. Gray said sunlight faded the furniture.

Ronnie dashed into the room, falling to his knees, sliding to a stop on the oak floor. He was my oldest and awfully cute, with big brown eyes, cowlick forever sticking up, enormous grin, two front teeth still a little big for his face. Already nine years old.

"Mama!," he exclaimed, kissing my cheek. "I got something to show you!" Galloping to his room, he darted back with a model airplane held high as though in flight, skidding again on his knees. "Look Mama! I finished the B-24 Liberator! A bomber!" I studied the model, proud because it seemed like something a much older boy would build. I believe my son worked harder making his model planes than his lazy father, my former husband, Vince Gray had ever worked at *anything*.

Mrs. Gray emerged from the kitchen bearing a tray holding an ornate silver coffee pot and a plate of molasses cookies. She set the tray on the coffee table. I was taken, as always, with the tiny spoons meant only for stirring coffee, and those delicate plates and cups with the little matching cream pitcher, all in the exquisite Desert Rose pattern. Mrs. Gray used these for everyday, bringing out her fine china for Sundays and other occasions. I would have beautiful things, too, someday.

BY THE TIME Vince Gray and I split up, we had two children: Ronnie, two years, and Linda, eight months. I was panicked about money. I had heard of some divorced fathers sending money every paycheck to help with the children, often only until the expenses of a new family ended it. I would never get a penny from Vince Gray, who worked by fits and starts, depending on money from his mother. How would I provide for my children? The only job for a woman around that desolate little Ozark town was waitressing for thirty cents an hour at the Highway Café. The pay would cover rent and utilities, but not enough left for groceries. Vince Gray suggested Ronnie live with Mrs. Gray until I got on my feet. That's what happened: my son went to live with his grandmother (breaking my heart), and my daughter and I moved in with my parents. I was crestfallen returning to the farm, which I had escaped at age eighteen by marrying Vince Gray, that smooth-talking twenty-five year old who turned out only to be a good-for-nothing.

"MRS. GRAY, I HAVE HAPPY NEWS!" Her expression was cordial, as always. "Remember when I told you in January how I met a man named Gil? After four months we get along great, and we will marry in a few days."

Mrs. Gray turned toward my son and spoke in her serene voice. "Ronald, honey." He looked up from examining his plane. "Your mother and I have things to talk about. Please go to your room. You may take one more cookie and your milk."

I was trembling. I needed a cigarette, but had never smoked in front of Mrs. Gray; she disapproved of women using tobacco.

Ronnie's door closed with a click.

"Mrs. Gray, I'll finally be settled and I can take my son home." Forcing a chuckle, I uttered words I had imagined would give Mrs. Gray a little laugh: "I guess I'm giving you notice!" She brushed the remark aside.

"Ellen, as I recall, you abandoned Ronald." That awful word, in such a refined, agreeable voice. "I took on your duties year after year, and became quite attached to the child after his grandfather died."

The room was suddenly depleted of oxygen. I tried to take some deep breaths as Mrs. Gray continued, her words betraying her pleasant expression.

"I will not allow you to take my innocent Ronald to some hovel with a husband who could well turn out to be a drunkard, as was your second."

I could not get my breath. "But, Mrs. Gray, you and Vince said you'd keep him until I got on my feet."

"Child, I was talking about a few months." My stomach clenched. "You got yourself re-married, then divorced at breakneck speed, jaunted off to Kansas City for two years, leaving three children farmed out to grandparents," her voice tranquil, as though at a church picnic on a lovely spring day.

"Mrs. Gray, I'll have a husband. I want my son with me!"

THE INK HAD NOT DRIED on my second marriage certificate when I realized my heavy-drinking bridegroom had no intention of stopping, even though he had assured me that with the support of a good wife, he would give up liquor just like that, no problem. That brief marriage left me with another baby, a little boy I named David. After we divorced, I had no choice but to go back again to my parents' farmhouse with Linda and David. I was miserable, hopeless of ever having my own place with all three children. In desperation, I soon decided to try my luck in Kansas City.

MRS. GRAY, unmoved by my exhortation, said, "Ellen, Ronald will continue to live with me, just as he has since he was two years old."

Ears ringing, hands shaking, I protested, "But, you don't understand! I'm his mother!

With frightful voice, Mrs. Gray fired back, "Ellen, it is you who does not understand. You are an unfit mother. Any court would agree." Her face, now an angry squall, "Almost immediately after your divorce from Vincent became final, you went and married that—that drunk!"

She glanced toward Ronnie's room, and paused. She softened her voice. "Think about it, my dear. There were not quite two years between Linda and your third child, born of separate marriages."

I was mortified.

"You left your children scattered all over the countryside while you cavorted off to Kansas City, got into only God knows what mischief."

"But, Mrs. Gray, it was the war, and it was in Kansas City that I was able to find a job that *paid* something and could save money for me and the kids. I took the seven-hour bus ride home to see them the first weekend of every month. You remember, right? When all the soldiers came home after V-J Day and the women lost their jobs, I came straight back to work at the café."

IT WAS after returning from Kansas City that I first met Gil when he strolled into the café one morning on my shift. He was visiting his parents, who had moved to Hillview from Kentucky. Our eyes met and he threw a smile in my direction. He was as handsome as Clark Gable, and I couldn't stop watching as he made his way to the counter. My heart pounded, and I wondered if this might be the real thing. After serving him coffee and eggs, I learned that he had been discharged from the Army after serving a while stateside following heavy combat in New Guinea. We flirted pretty good, and he asked me out for a beer. We had been dating ever since.

Gil had been able to find only day work in Hillview, but my heart told me this marriage would be different. Jobs were scarce in that beggarly town in the Missouri Ozarks, but Gil was a worker. He would find regular employment. He had already spent long days fixing up our sorry rental bungalow—three rooms, a bare light bulb in the center of each room operated with a pull string, a hand pump at the kitchen sink supplying water, and a galvanized tub hanging on the wall for baths. There was a privy out back. Our love would brighten the pitiable dwelling, making it feel like a mansion. I knew that one day Gil would give me everything I dreamed of: a house that people would admire, just as I admired Mrs. Gray's; a new car in the garage; and the family wearing store-bought clothing sent out to be washed and ironed.

MY WORDS MATTERED NO MORE to Mrs. Gray than the buzz of that fly. "Ellen, I knew this day would come. I consulted my lawyer as soon as you went prancing off to Kansas City."

Face now composed, voice agreeable, "You do not have a leg to stand on, my dear, what with abandoning Ronald, much less if we would, regrettably, have to present the unfit mother aspect."

My chest ached. There was no way I could pay a lawyer; and no judge would ever see my side once Mrs. Gray's attorney pointed out my three kids had two fathers, that I had been divorced twice by the time I turned twenty-seven, and that I had not provided a home for any of my children from the time of my first divorce at age twenty-one.

"You may continue to visit, of course." she pronounced.

I was dizzy and trembling with heartache and grief.

"Ellen, have you never wondered why I did not offer to take Linda, as well?"

Her eyes flashed towards Ronnie's door, and, not waiting for my answer, she slowly

hissed, "Because Vincent revealed to me he didn't think Linda was his. *That's* why I didn't take her."

So low and nasty. I was proud that I did not crumple into tears. There was a brief silence.

"Under the circumstances, Ellen, I think you will prefer to let yourself out."

Stricken, tears trapped inside, I gathered myself, and not looking again toward Mrs. Gray, nor speaking, I slipped into the entryway, pushed open the heavy walnut door, and escaped Mrs. Gray's dark house into the brightness of day. Birds flitted in the trees, chirping as though nothing had happened, as if everything about this day was normal.

I DO NOT REMEMBER GETTING into the car, but there I was, stunned. The car rumbled to life, tailpipe belching ash-colored billows. I tried not to think about Mrs. Gray's hateful words—calling me an adulteress, saying I abandoned my son.

Driving the fifteen miles home on curving Highway 60, I smoked constantly, chaining one to the next. I needed to cry in Gil's arms, tell him what had happened, what was said, feel his love and sympathy. I thought how ladies simply do not say the foul things I thought I heard Mrs. Gray say. She was a lady, a dignified lady. I must have imagined those words, for if she had truly said them, how could I ever go back to that house, even to visit my son? Then, a fearful thought: what if sharing Mrs. Gray's detestable words would cause Gil to wonder? What if he turned against me?

There was the blast of a car horn and sudden awareness that my car was straddling the center line. I forced the heavy vehicle back into my lane of the twisting road. I began sobbing. I remembered that I failed to hug Ronnie good-bye. I did not tell him I would be back for another visit soon.

A TRIP TO THE BANK

ALICE LANDRUM

The jangle of the phone interrupted Eleanor as she scrambled eggs for the breakfast of her two teen daughters, both upstairs getting ready for school.

"Eleanor, it's Robert."

"How are you, Hon? Where are you?"

"I'm in Des Moines. The farm machinery show starts in an hour. I called now because I need for you to take that deposit to the bank this morning."

"I see it here on the desk."

From the pile of documents and letters on Robert's steel-gray metal desk, she picked up an envelope labeled as Deposit for the Lewisville Bank and stowed it in her tote bag.

After finishing breakfast with the girls, she headed for the carport.

Eleanor directed her white sedan away from the Kentucky farm-house where she had raised five children with her husband, Robert, a farmer, and board member at the local bank in Lewisville. As she drove, she thought with pride of her husband's position at the bank and of what she and her husband had accomplished in the community, but she also felt underappreciated. Here she was dropping a task at home to take care of this bank deposit. The garden would have to wait. She hoped that rain didn't come today before she was able to set out the tomato plants.

She steered the car slowly south on the narrow blacktop road that climbed a gentle hill. At the top of the hill, if she stopped to look back, she could see the red cattle barn, the farmhouse with its white painted chimney on the south end, the windmill next to the pond, the faded pine tobacco barn, the tenant's house on the hill to the north, the green sprouts of corn in the field to the east, and the rocky pastureland to the south with the white-faced red Hereford cattle scattered across the field. But on this spring day in June 1980, she did not look back. Robert had insisted that she deposit the check as soon as the bank opened that morning.

Her sedan passed the Tompkins' house, a two-story home covered with native stone. The Tompkins family had lived in that house for more than one hundred years. When she reached an intersection, she turned right in the direction of Lewisville only three miles away.

She drove past another field of corn sprouting through the dark earth and then arrived at the intersection with the old highway that used to be the main east to west road connecting the larger towns in western Kentucky. She turned left and arrived at the outer edge of Lewisville where only a half mile away the bank sat surrounded by maple and oak trees on another low hill in the center of town. The gently rolling terrain in this farm community provided an ideal base for the cultivation of crops like corn, wheat, and soybeans.

The bank handled the accounts for all the local farmers who came there for deposits and withdrawals and for loans when needed to buy the seed and supplies for the planting of the next crops. The bank board acted as the final judge of who would survive the risky business of farming subject to the whims of weather and markets.

Eleanor guided the sedan into the parking lot at the rear of the bank building, a one-story red brick structure. There were three other vehicles in the lot. She recognized Tom Woodward's station wagon, a beige and white vehicle. Tom served as the bank manager. Eleanor graduated from high school with Tom many years ago. One of the other vehicles, a small blue Beetle Volkswagen, belonged to Betty Sue

Smith who had worked as a teller in the bank for twenty years. But the dusty black Chevy with a dent in the right front fender did not belong to anyone that Eleanor knew.

She left her vehicle and started up the concrete steps to the back door. When she tugged the handle on the door, it would not open. When she peered through the thick glass into the hall, there was no one there but it was not uncommon for the people who worked there to be up front in the main lobby dealing with customers either at desks or behind the teller windows. However, she did feel uneasy. Normally that door swung open easily during the hours that the bank was open to the public.

Walking around the building through the grass, she decided to enter at the front entrance that faced Main Street. When she reached the front steps, she went up to the door with the words Lewisville Bank emblazoned in gold outlined with black. She tried to pull the door open, but this door also resisted her tug. Peering through the glass, she saw on the floor outstretched legs with shoe tops pointed up to the ceiling. Her eyes followed the legs to the bodies of two middle-aged women and an older man, all dressed in their usual business clothing, the women in floral print dresses and the man in gray slacks with a white shirt. His dark tie fell to one side of his prominent belly.

As she stared with alarm, her legs felt weak, and her heart started to pound in her chest. What had happened to these people? Had they been shot? She couldn't see any blood.

As she continued to peer through the glass at the tellers' windows, she saw a man with a black hood over his head and a black pistol in his right hand. In his left hand he held out a canvas bag into which the bank manager dropped multiple bundles of banknotes. Then the hooded man turned away and ran down the hall toward the back lot.

She looked back at the people on the floor. The woman closest to the door turned her head and saw Eleanor who recognized Betty Sue. Betty Sue mouthed the word "Help."

Eleanor signaled to Betty Sue that she understood and then turned away to run across the lawn down the hill across the street to the Quik

Trip. As she ran, her feet twisted on the uneven lawn, but she kept going.

She rushed out of breath into the store where she saw Dennis, a middle-aged male clerk at the counter. He stood behind the cash register dressed in a yellow shirt topped with a red vest. His shaggy brown hair touched his ears and Eleanor could see some dark stubble on his chin. An aroma of cigarette smoke hung in the air around him.

"Dennis, there's a robbery at the bank. Call the sheriff."

"Oh, Eleanor, that can't be. I ain't heard anything about a robbery." She could see that Dennis resented a woman telling him what to do.

"Dennis, I was just there. The doors are locked, and people are lying on the floor. A hooded man ran out the back with a bag full of bills."

"Eleanor, you are just pulling my leg." He turned away to wait on another customer, a man who had walked in after Eleanor.

She felt crushed. She stood still her feet glued to the concrete floor. As she looked down, her thoughts raced. Why didn't he believe her? Was it because she was a middle-aged red headed female? Did he resent her husband who recently turned him down for a loan?

In the distance they heard the piercing wail of a police car siren. The wailing came closer.

Dennis turned toward the sound and then back to Eleanor with a sheepish look in his eyes.

"I guess something must be going on up at the bank," he admitted.

With her head raised, Eleanor took a big breath and gave him a smile. She would come back to the bank on a different day to make the deposit.

As she turned to walk out the door, she heard Dennis call after her, "Eleanor, do you want a free cup of coffee?"

"No thank you, Dennis."

Later after she learned that the robber had not hurt any of the people on the floor at the bank, she shared the day's events on the phone with Robert who observed with a laugh, "That's why Dennis didn't get the loan."

1428: MESSAGE IN A BOTTLE

LISA ADAMS-LLOYD

You may not have heard of me, but around here I'm kind of a big deal. And although my story is interesting and tragic in its own right, that's not the reason I've put this message in a bottle. If you are reading this, we need your help!

There is no time to waste, but first things first. My name is Adelaide. I'm one of the last surviving Hawksbill turtles living off the coast of the Faroe Islands. In the hopeful chance you're willing to act, it's good to know this North Atlantic archipelago is situated between Iceland and the Shetland Islands.

As for me, I'm forty-three-years-old and the way things are going I may not be around for very much longer. You see, things in these parts are changing fast and we're in danger. I'm sending this out in hopes that someone will hear my SOS.

Please know I appreciate any hesitancy you might feel after reading this. I, too, found it hard to believe the stories stewing about the seven seas. But let me reassure you, I can attest that my own tale is one-hundred-percent true. So, grant me patience to help you get a feel for what's been happening and why your help is urgently needed.

Members of our sea life community are spitting out stories that until recently, most — like me, haven't given much credence. But so shocking was what I witnessed that I think there may actually be something to all this testimony.

From microscopic to mammoth, sea creatures are experiencing inexplicable bouts of illness and disease. From coral to mammal and plankton to whale, our community is succumbing one-by-one to our ailing seas. We used to be a thronging set of marine life, full of vigor with a top bill of health. Sadly, that's no longer the case.

Some blame the spills; others blame the runoff. I can't disagree with either. By now most of us have figured out to avoid the "funny" colored and foul-tasting areas but still, sickness persists. Why just the other day, I met a gray seal complaining of a terrible headache. I didn't have the heart to tell him he had a huge growth sprouting on his head. Many others are complaining of fertility issues, and some are just plain starving. It's really quite tragic.

Then there are the increasing cases of fish-napping. Reports are coming in from all over the seas that huge numbers of fish are disappearing after being tangled in nets. I hear the message boards across the Eastern Australian Current, are covered in "missing" posters.

There is also talk of an island (the size of Texas? I'm told) floating in the Pacific made entirely of trash. My friend Nosa swears by her cousin's account. According to her, there is a super swirling of plastic and paper fibers thickened into a toxic soup by something she termed, "micro-plastics." She claims it's choking off the entire supply chain.

Well, it was all just too far fetched to believe, if you ask me. I wanted to give my friends favor but denied it all, dismissing it as just casual rumors and chitchat. That is, until I saw the most shocking thing before my very own eyes.

This is the story from which I can personally attest and why we need your help straight away. It was the twelfth of September in the year of twenty-twenty-one. I remember because I ran into Bennie that morning and it was his birthday. It was a beautiful Fall day. The sun was shining, the water cool and crystal clear and the current strong to my liking.

I was busy munching on sea sponges when a huge pod of white-sided dolphins swam overhead. A pair of passing sisters whistled then waved a flipper to me. When I grinned and motioned for them to visit, they dove greeting me with a series of clicks. These young-uns, Rosemary and Clementine, had polished round noses, sunny faces and wore a cape of dark gray over their white under-sided bodies. Fast swimmers, they reported to be heading towards cooler waters that fateful morning.

All the while we chatted, I drifted, admiring their *joie de vivre*. They were such carefree characters, exhibiting such joy and spirit! After warning the girls of the large tangle of ghost fishing gear I spotted floating on the surface the previous day, they begged their leave, anxious to return to the safety of the pod. I bid them good day, then resumed my meal in peace.

Soon after their departure I heard a familiar roar overhead. The sun was shielded by sea foam and moving dark shadows approached. Before I could blink, I saw Rosemary and Clementine — along with friends and family, nudging each other in a high-spirited game of chase. There were other creatures getting in on the fun, too. Chasing, bumping and muscling my dear friends.

I decided to stay put, steering clear of the commotion. Priding myself as a sensible turtle, I knew being mixed up the middle of a race was no place for a girl like me. And I was sure to hear the grand tale from my newest friends another day.

My friend Zeddy, a fifty-five-year-old leatherback, paddled by about that time. What he said shocked me. He explained the roar was not the rush of our friends racing but of small boats filled with anglers chasing. Chasing whom? I naturally asked.

That was when he told me the most heinous tale. Now, as I've said, I've been around a while but never have I heard of any atrocity like the one he told. He cautioned me from following my friends, for fear that I might meet my own demise. Surely, you exaggerate, I protested. But no, he promised what he said was true.

I'll never forget his words as he told me of over 65,000 dolphins and small whales being senselessly killed in recent memory. Humans, he explained, billed it "*The Grind*." Each season, a gathering of "thrill-seekers," (his words, mind you) chase large pods of whales and dolphins into the ground. Why, when he told me his account, I must admit being dumbstruck, and filled with fear.

Aghast with horror, I immediately began fretting over my new friends' well-being. But Zeddy cautioned against any involvement on my part. He said even if I could catch up with them, I would likely become ensnared in my own bloody ending.

Trembling, I listened while he shared more details. Can you imagine? I gasped. Our seafaring friends are run aground then left choking for breath, he told. Oddly reminiscent of our old school textbooks warning about becoming packed like sardines in a can, the dolphin lie side by side on the sandy coast writhing in pain. Then, he exclaimed, as if trying to be the heroes, the evildoers put the poor dears "out of their misery."

Naturally — and regretfully, I asked what he meant. He explained the dolphin and whale are hacked to death by hooks and hatchets. Shamefully I admit, I lost my lunch right there and then. Surely there is something we can do? I pleaded. But Zeddy just shook his head.

I was shellshocked as you can imagine, floating numb until I was stirred by a group of schooling herring which were passing by. Also roused by their intrusion was a camouflaged angel shark lurking beneath me at the bottom.

Revived from my stupor, I knew I needed to act. I had to stop this game of treachery before any other whale or dolphin was hurt. I swam like hell, giving every pull everything I had. Quickly I realized it wasn't enough. I sent out a call to hitch a ride. The angel shark answered as I begged for his help.

The words I tell next are distressing, heartbreaking really. You'll want to stop reading now, but I press you to go on. As the light lifted bright and water grew shallow, I felt a harrowing clang in my gut. The tidal backwash greeting me was stained pink, deepening to red and smelling of salty sulfur.

My stomach dropped. I tugged on my ride to slow his efforts and jumped off his back — forgetting my manners to thank him, in the process. My mouth fell open as I broke the surface. On the beach lay my friends with one thousand, four-hundred and twenty-six of their family — left gasping and gutted.

1428 souls lie still in the sand

I swear by Neptune, my words are true. Each season in Taiji, Japan and the Faroe Islands, dolphins, whales, and others are hunted for sport in the name of tradition. Please, I implore you to spread the word and demand a stop to this godless killing. We all play small but far-reaching roles in the master plan. Each fracture in the chain of life hurts the whole and our future. Please help by raising your voice and being mindful of your habits and choices. Love, Addy

THE GORY DETAILS

YOLANDA CIOLLI

The cattle-trodden path deepened and narrowed until we were forced to walk heel to toe in the single shoe width track. Marching down the hill in the hot sun, the four of us reached the edge of the creek and stepped into the cool water in the shaded edge of the woods.

"Let's go, Ellen. Dave, keep moving. It's a long haul to the North Woods. And up hill, too." Don prodded us younger kids, and always lied about it when we told on him. Don had seven years on Jane, who was ten, with me at nine, and Dave at eight.

"You don't have to be so bossy! We aren't in a hurry anyway. You told us this walk was just for fun," I said. "You could let us have a minute to cool off."

Don frowned and gave a sardonic look.

Dave let out a shriek when Don pinched him on the thigh. "Ow! That hurt, Don. Why do you have to always be so mean?"

"When I have to watch you kids, I do whatever I need to keep you in line. Mom told me to make sure you minded."

Jane, the oldest of us younger three finally pitched in, "Well you don't have to be such an asshole, Don. Dave wasn't doing anything."

"That's just the point. He's supposed to be moving along."

"We always stop here," I said. "The spring is cool and we want to get a drink."

Don shot an evil look at me. "Well, Ellen, maybe you should hurry Dave along before you get a good pinch too."

Jane and I shut up and took our turns getting a drink from the spring, then pulled Dave along to follow Don, who had already taken off. Don's long stride left us practically running to catch up.

We passed the pond ahead and saw Don had gone east toward the old pump. "Don! Don!" we shouted in turns. He turned around and waved us forward. There was no choice left but to run.

When we got there, out of breath and sweaty, Don was pumping the handle, trying to pull up water from the old cistern well. "Good; you're finally here. Jane, you pump now," Don ordered.

Jane took the handle and kept at it. Pretty soon a trickle started, then the rusty water gushed out. When the water cleared, Don stuck his head under, then shook his head like the dog he was. "This is how you cool off," he said.

Dave followed Don's example and dunked his head in the flow of the gushing water, and his small face came up with a smile. "Yeah, this is good," he said.

Jane, champion Girl Scout that she was, was still pumping away, but clearly tiring out. "Ellen, it's your turn now. Keep the water coming so I can cool down, too." She dipped her head into the water while I labored away.

"Jane, we should see if they have a Scout badge for pumping water from a well," I said. "I want my sash to be covered with badges."

Don rolled his eyes and said, "Let's get going again. You guys are wasting too much time."

"You're the one who left the path to come to the pump," Dave chimed in.

"That's right, and we are going to stay off the path. I've decided to go over to the Gilbert's fence over there." Don pointed to the east and added, "Either come on or I'll give you another good pinch. Mom will honk the horn if we are late."

Dave winced and started trudging behind him, and Jane and I took up the rear.

"That doggone Don," Jane mumbled. "We're supposed to be back by three o'clock. We'll never make it. When Mom finds out where he took us, she's going to be really mad. I hope she makes him do dishes for a month."

"That would only happen if Don owns up to the fact. Remember the last time we thought he was going to get in trouble, he lied and we got blamed. We were the ones who did dishes," I said. "Mom always lets her precious Don get away with murder."

"You guys stop your muttering," Don said over his shoulder. He couldn't hear what we were saying, but he knew we weren't happy about the turn of events.

The place we were headed was a lot farther than the North Woods. There was no path, so we waded along through the tall grass until we got to the fence. Just beyond the three-foot wire was a huge black Angus bull.

"Come on, you go first," Don said to us.

"I'm not going." Jane stood her ground, and me and Dave followed suit.

"I'm scared of cows." I was not going either.

Dave cowered behind me and we all three backed away.

"Then I'll go by myself." Don hoisted himself up and over the fence. The bull was staring at him, and Don stared back.

"You better come back," Jane said. "That looks like a mean bull."

Don took a step toward the bull.

"Don't, Don," I warned.

The bull stood still, but didn't take his eyes off Don.

"We should go back. I think I hear Mom honking the horn," Dave said. "I'm scared."

Don turned to face us. "You guys are all chicken."

The bull snorted and stamped. Jane shouted, "Watch out, Don!"

By the time Don turned back around the bull had made a run for him. All I could do was cover my eyes. While Don was scrambling over the fence, the bull grazed his side with his horn.

"Oh my God!" Jane shrieked, pushing me and Dave back with her arms. Jane did her best to help Don over the fence, but he was hurt. In the distance, we all heard the car horn for real. Don was white-faced with terror and bleeding through his ripped shirt, but still we were running through the grass for fear that the bull would bust through the fence.

We made it back to the house in record time, and Mom was mad. That is, until she saw the ripped and blood-soaked shirt on Don. She got the story out of him, and for once he didn't lie. He knew Mom would be sympathetic. With a pale face, she loaded him in the car and took him to Dr. Fulks's office. Jane, Dave and I stayed home with our older sister, Cindy.

Cindy had overheard the story about the bull already, but we tattled to her about Don's bullying us the whole time we were on the walk.

In the end, Don got the wound cleaned and dressed, along with a tetanus shot at the doctor's office. He got lots of sympathy from Mom, until at supper when she heard the rest of the tale. She gave him a lecture about setting a bad example and being mean to us kids—in front of the whole family. And she grounded him from using the family car for two weeks. We were glad.

I thought Mom let Don off easy, but we added to his punishment by telling and re-telling the story of how Don "the bully" got the bull he deserved. And we didn't spare any gory details.

RAIN

KAREN MOCKER DABSON

Delicious.

To be captured on such a day by a sudden rainstorm.

Daisy watched the drip-drops bounce all around her as she stood neck deep in the pond. They mesmerized her. Their steady cadence pattered the water. Each drop spoke, nearly inaudibly, practically sighing their tiny splish-plops.

She liked the way the drops would jump up again, as though the water burned to the touch. And how they centered themselves perfectly, each time, within their own splash zone, a circle of miniature wave that expanded until it bumped into the next circle, and the next.

The symphony of the raindrops was all she wanted, all she needed to leave the bad times behind.

COMFORT ZONE

STEVE C. FRIEDMAN

A 16-mile training run didn't seem as daunting as the stare down Henry was receiving from the five-month-old orange and white tabby cat purring away on his lap.

"I actually let one of these things into my house?" Henry thought to himself as Comet stretched out his steely paws, yawned his spike-lined mouth, and further settled into content cat nap mode.

Henry acknowledged that he personally agreed this was the autumn to leave his comfort zone. What he mostly meant though was his setting sites on a full marathon – 26.2 miles – instead of the "feeble" half marathons he had always entered. It would take a clear mindset to double the distance, he thought, and conquer a nagging goal.

But if running a marathon was Henry's desire, his wife had dwelt on her urge to get a cat for more than a decade. Anna had been dissuaded by Henry for most of their marriage about getting a feisty fang-riddled fuzzball with a penchant for rodentia homicide.

"You don't know if you're allergic."

"What, and have our stuff all scratched up?"

"You want an open air cat crap box in our house?"

"I hear they suck people's souls out."

Henry's thirteen years of excuses and incoherent blatherings were finally wearing Anna out. Even nine-year-old daughter Kate had enough. Her teary-eyed persuasive essay – complete with drawings of a girl hugging a cat – had gone unheeded for months.

"I'm nine! You know how many of my friends don't have pets at this age? Zero!" ranted the frustrated fourth grader.

"You know how many of your friends at this age can't ride bikes? Zero!" Henry shot back. "You work on perfecting that and maybe we'll talk about a cat!"

Lo and behold, Kate did perfect the bike. Rode it so damn good after three lessons she was making tight left-hand turns in a church parking lot.

"What about that cat now?" Kate asked.

"Well, we'll think about it," said Henry, which of course meant no.

"Ugh!"

Yet here it was several weeks later and Comet had wormed his way into the family's collective heart. Henry contemplated the chain of weekend events that brought the nutless wonder into their abode.

===

The 0.5 mile marker on the City Trail was just a few feet away. "Crap, I've got to pee," thought Henry. Luckily, a clump of trees and bushes down a nearby embankment provided the quick download shelter he needed before embarking on his endeavor.

The late Saturday afternoon sky was starting to clear after heavy early autumn rains. It was perfect 50 degree weather for to bag the white whale that had been taunting Henry since he became interested in running.

The gravel and dust lined City Trail stretched for more than 8 miles before depositing into a much larger state maintained trail. "Down and back, 16 miles, how hard can it be?" Henry thought. Easy to imagine, but when 13.1 miles had been his previous furthest distance, the extra three miles might as well have been to Mars.

To compound the problem, Henry had been running on the trail for half his life. There were no surprises. There's the hulking steel frame of the old railroad bridge around 3.5, the walnut tree with a perfect C shape in its otherwise straight trunk at 5.0, the water treatment plant with its blaring phone siren at 6.5, and the winding creek littered with empty car chassis along its bank at 8.0. "Hard to leave a comfort zone when it's all familiar territory," he thought.

Yet he clicked the start button on his Garmin and proceeded to put one foot in front of the other, mile after mile, kicking up tiny limestone pebbles as he went. Same bridge, same tree, same blaring phone, same rusted chassis, and then 8.5, his half way mark. "Alright, let's shred these last bastards!" Henry shouted to no one in particular.

While he was expecting a rougher time back, the time and miles clicked off faster than anticipated. A rude biker almost ended the running nirvana, nearly clipping Henry coming out of a turn. He recovered, stared down the remaining stretch of semi-infinite trail span and returned to the very spot he had left from two and a half hours earlier.

All Henry could do was raise his hands in solo glory, no one around to share in his accomplishment. Back at his truck he typed out a frenetic text to Anna between gulps of Gatorade: "Did it! 16.0 freakin' miles! Ready for more!"

Back home, Anna's phone came alive with the message. While happy for her husband, she immediately looked over at Kate and said, "Hey, we're going to go get a cat tomorrow."

===

The event was billed as Match-a-Thon. Area pet shelters brought their spade and neutered dogs and cats to a musty horse ring to pair pets with people. After filling out some paperwork, Anna was handed a purple card and told to show her color to the handlers.

"We're just looking," came out of her mouth for the fifth time that day. Kate nodded her head to her dad, then slyly exchanged looks with her mom.

"Just like a used car – kick a few tires, look under the hood…" said Henry.

"Look, you could of stayed home and watched football," Anna said. "Kate and I have known about this for weeks. Just humor us, okay?"

"Fine."

Anna banked on a hunch that Henry would be more pliable after having completed his goal. She knew the event would take the guess work out finding the right pet.

"Ah, purple, well come this way," said the jovial handler whose jacket was covered in animal hair. "These purple types are curious and enjoy people but they also enjoy their own space just as much. Social, but to a point."

All Henry could see was a mass of caged fur, some licking paws and grooming themselves ("Disgusting."), some stretching after a long nap ("Real industrious."), some using the little cardboard box in the corner to do their business ("What a selling point."). The handler opened up one cage and produced a three-month short hair with a splotch of white on its black coat and all-white paws.

"This one is Fluffs, because, well you get the idea," the handler said. "He's possibly the cutest kitten we have left."

"Oh Dad, Mom!" Kate said, heart melting as Fluffs was placed in her waiting hands. Kate gently stroked the cat's head and ears. Cute yes, but Fluffs didn't seem like the cat. His lack of purring showed that he was all looks, no substance.

This was Anna's show after all. While acknowledging Kate's response to the animal, she was driving this bus. "He's a cute one sweetie, but let's keep looking. You don't want to fall in love with the first one you see."

Purple cat after purple cat were handed to Anna and Kate but none seemed to have the "it" quality. Henry was starting to feel good about the just looking stance when they came to the last set of cages. Comet sat alert in his cage next to his black-and-white haired sister. Sporting a mostly white under carriage with orange spots on his face and back, Comet looked out from his cage and emitted an inquisitive "Mew?"

"Oh, this one wants to know how you're doing," the handler saw. "Maybe this is finally the one for you."

Sinking into Anna arms, rapid-fire purring commenced. Comet was visibly nervous yet content as well. "Well aren't you a pretty kitty," Anna cooed.

"But Mom, Fluffs is a much cuter…" Kate started.

"I don't know Kate, this one looks like a keeper," said Anna, pushing her motherly will and Comet into Kate's arms.

"Oh, I see what you mean!" Kate said. "This one purrs like crazy. Dad, here, take him!"

"That's okay, you do your thing," said Henry, coming to terms that a thunderbolt had just struck and there was no going back to just looking stage.

Before he knew it, Henry saw hand shakes being made, cardboard cat carriers being readied and yet more paperwork completed. All that was left was to get an adoption picture with family and new feline.

Comet was already rattling around in the pet carrier unaware of his new circumstances, leaving the shelter of cage and sister.

"You mind getting your cat out?" the photographer asked.

The lid was open and out popped the anxious cat, evading capture and scouting potential hiding spots around the horse rink. Henry's instinctive running skills took over, cornering the jittery Comet only to get an arm and shoulder full of claws.

"You feel you left your comfort zone now?" Anna asked as the awkward family photo was taken.

"You know," said Henry, looking into Comet's yellow eyes, bonding over pain. "It can't hurt losing my soul to this little guy. Certainly not any worse than these scratches."

A LIFE MADE FOR HER

KATHY GAN

She touched the wine glass carefully while staring at the door of the Italian restaurant and knew this would be difficult. She focused so hard on the door and practiced in her mind the words she'd say. Tonight, she'd stand her ground, say the words needed to end this relationship that had mapped out her entire life in a direction she did not want. She wanted more out of life, and she was going to get it. Emmet dashed through the door and began greeting everyone. There were smiles all around her and it was at that moment she noticed the crowd. It was family, friends, and co-workers. Before she knew what was happening, Emmet was on one knee, and she was saying yes. Yes, to a life she didn't want.

THE BANDANA

THOMAS HERSKOWITZ

"It feels hotter at this altitude. The peak is over 14,505 ft. Almost there!" He drew the cotton square from his back pocket, shook it open, wiped his brow and then blew his nose into it. The twelve-year-old boy strained under the backpack. He grimaced, disgusted by the sight of the man's action.

"That is so gross."

"What? This?" The man folded the blue and white paisley cotton fabric, being careful to line up the folds. It ended up as a square the size of his hand. "This, my son, is a multi-tool. It's a handkerchief, a cool towel, a shade, a bandage or a tourniquet. It's whatever I want it to be. But what it is not, is gross. You know what makes it not gross?"

"What?"

"The order of operation." He placed his hand upon the boy's shoulder. "If you noticed, I wiped and then blew. Then I put it away. It'll dry before I need it again."

"It's still gross."

"Well..." He moved his palm from the shoulder to his son's cheek. "**This** hand touched my snot rag and now **it** lies upon your face." He tapped his fingers twice on his son's cheek and then slowly wiped his palm across his face.

"Ewww, Dad!" he smiled as he pushed his father's hand away. They both laughed and set out the trail again.

"Since this is your first backpack trip, there are some things that we need to make you look the part. First things first, you need your own kerchief." He pulled a black bandana with white paisleys out and tossed it to his son. "This is yours now. Open it and fold it into a triangle, then tie it around your neck."

The young man did as his dad asked. "I'm not gonna blow my nose into it. That's just not gonna happen."

"We shall see." He turned and led them further up the trail. "Keep an eye out for a good walking stick. It should be as straight as possible, strong, and between your chest and shoulder tall"

As they paused to fill their canteens, the father spotted it. "Tommy, look at this one." He hopped across the stream and grabbed the gnarled branch thick with branches at one end. The thickest end of the branch ended where it was rent from the tree, the tear was shaped like a wave.

"It's too big. It's taller than you" the boy rejected it outright.

"I will make it work. You use mine, while I whittle this into the perfect walking stick." He reached out his walking stick, the boy grabbed it and pulled him back across the stream with his prize: A giant branch.

The boy poked his hand through the leather lanyard on his father's walking stick, grabbed hold of the staff and began marching up the trail. His dad dragged the branch behind him, whittling off the branches and producing a nice thick branch.

By the time they had reached the summit, it had become an 8-foot branch shaped like a carrot with a wave at the big end. His father tied his bandana to the small end and waved it like a flag back and forth like a conquering hero.

SAD SEX IN VEGAS, BAD DRUGS IN VERMONT

MARY HORNER

"I know all about this one," the man said as he approached me. He held out his right hand so I shook it. I had nothing to say.

"I'm Ray."

"Oh, Ray. The Ray?" I said, with a slight bit of sarcasm, which I could get away with because of loud music and a generous bartender.

"Yes ... that's right."

Smiling, he shook my hand with more enthusiasm.

I had no clue. I was familiar to him. I knew by the way he looked at me. I felt self conscious quickly. I don't know if it was because I didn't know him and was supposed to, or that he knew me, but I didn't know why.

He leaned in close, with his mouth inches away from my right ear. His low voice filled my head with the smooth richness of jazz music on a rainy night. Every sentence ended with a sly smile. He liked to know where he stood with everyone, but mostly, he liked to get inside and stay there.

Ray was about my height, probably a little taller, with brown hair and eyes and a goatee. His eye contact was steady, but it went beyond that. He stared me down like a seventh grader trying to establish territory, not afraid to look the devil in the eye. I lost the "who would blink first" competition. He won because he was prepared to win. Every encounter for him is a situation to conquer. He doesn't let his guard down. He's a player, a dealer. Everyone knows that. Everyone, except me.

According to Ray, people are classified into alpha dogs or omega dogs with nothing in between. He wasn't interested in what was lost in the middle, and I was omega with a capital "O". I wouldn't really register on his radar screen until later that night.

When he took his eyes off me, he turned them to Rudy and shook his hand like old friends. Rudy is my husband. We sat down at a table close to the pool table, away from the people who actually knew Melissa, the birthday girl. For most of the night, we talked to Steve and Linda, other peripheral friends from work. Our hosts fed us and gave us drinks anyway. Melissa pretended to care that we were there, which was sweet. She was turning 30, the fourth wife to Jerry, 11 years her senior.

The birthday girl's father made a sloppy toast to 30 years and raised his glass. We all raised our glasses and pretended that he was either less drunk, or we were more drunk, choosing to ignore the sad little man who called her Melinda. Melissa walked over to our table and told us her dad and mom might be getting back together.

"He slept at her house the night before," she said.

I didn't know if that was a good thing. I wasn't sure how to respond neutrally.

"Oh," is what I think I said, and nodded like I meant it.

On the wall behind the birthday cake was a bulletin board decorated with pink ribbon showing the birthday girl riding her tricycle on a street lined with mobile homes. I wondered if that was where she grew up, and if her parents slept together in one of those mobile homes the night before. Then I wondered why I wanted to know.

There wasn't much action on our side of the rented room, but it was better than the bar area. Several women, including a set of twins, danced nearby. I didn't know them, but I knew they were twins because they dressed alike -- dark black flared pants with slits on each leg at the bottom in the back. Their shirts were charcoal gray, and tight. I watched them dance sometimes, along with everyone else. They were beautiful. They looked like the kind of women who disappear during the week and come out only on weekends to be beautiful and envied and wanted.

Ray, on the other hand, was a mess, well, half a mess, anyway. He loved the wrong woman, had his own drug problem, and his shirt was pressed but his jeans were wrinkled. These were not just normal wrinkles from sitting in the dryer too long. More like a dog slept on them while they were wet. A big dog. Then the dog wore them to work every day for a week. When the dog came home on the last day, Ray put them on and left for Linda's party. That kind of wrinkled.

Ray didn't seem to care that he looked uneven, off kilter, even, with his pressed shirt and wrinkled pants that dragged the ground. He bought them in a longer length to pretend he was taller, like women buy clothes that are too small to pretend they are thinner. A few minutes after I met him he looked me over, like a car salesman looks over a new client, wondering how much money he has and what he'll have to do to get him to part with it. We were playing pool and my turn followed his in the lineup.

"Would you leave Rudy if you were sick?"

I stared at him and couldn't answer. When his turn came, he took it. I walked away.

Rudy and I played pool a couple times later, but we never danced. We haven't danced together since the 90s. Rudy was drinking so it was easier for him to be nice to me. He even offered to get me a drink once. I accepted.

"Red wine, please," I said.

"O.K.," he replied. "I'll be right back." Just like it says in the dating etiquette book from the 50s I found in the library.

When he came back with the wine, he told me about LeeAnn, the love of Ray's life. He talked to me like I was a friend. He asked me if I saw her, the skinny woman by the bar with the long brown hair and light blue sweater. I did.

"That's her, that's LeeAnn," he said. "Ray is hopelessly in love with her."

LeeAnn was talking to another man, a taller, thinner version of Ray with brown hair and a goatee. Probably younger, too. Ray watched them. When Melissa came by with a camera, Ray managed to get in the picture with LeeAnn and the other man. I figured he would get a copy, scan it and remove the other guy. At least, that's what I would do if I were him. Maybe that's just me.

A few times Ray spoke briefly to LeeAnn before she would back away. Once she even danced away, trying to fit in with the others near the bar. She was different, though. Her body didn't move the same way. She was more subdued and a bit awkward. She didn't move much from the waist up. Her wine almost spilled once during her dancing getaway, and Ray leapt to her like he could save the wine from falling from the glass, reversing gravity. He couldn't, though, because it didn't spill. He knew he overreacted because he looked around to see if anyone saw. I saw. Then he saw that I saw.

"Would you leave him," he silently mouthed the words to me from across the room. I stared at him and cocked my head to one side because I wanted to give his question serious consideration. I couldn't decide because I didn't know, so I shrugged my shoulders and shook my head.

Rudy told me Ray owned his own company, always had a fast car and would fly "girls" out to Vegas to impress them. I knew, because I've taken a psychology class, that he was just trying to find someone to help him stop loving LeeAnn. I thought about the nights in strange beds covered in soft sheets in expensive hotels. He was only with someone else to try to take the edge off the night and sadness of sleeping with someone who isn't LeeAnn.

I decided LeeAnn should love Ray back. Surely his love was enough for both of them. My plan was to follow her into the ladies' room and let her know how I felt. Before I had a chance, she slipped into the chair beside me and introduced herself. I introduced myself right back.

"I'm Christine," I said. She already knew who I was because she knew Rudy. She said they went to a football game together, although Rudy denied it.

Without hesitating, LeeAnn began telling me her history with Ray. They were together for 13 years, and married for 9. She left him a couple of years ago. So I told Rudy what she told me. I asked him if he knew. He shrugged, like he knew, but it didn't matter. Of course it mattered. That changed everything.

She said she was moving to Arizona in a few weeks. She wanted to live in the desert. Ray didn't know she was leaving for the second time.

"Her parents live in Cross Towers, near Phoenix, close to my folks," Rudy said. "In the big money section," he whispered quietly.

"Ray got hold of some bad drugs one night," she said. "Then he got hold of me. He planned a skiing trip in Vermont. The trip was supposed to make everything bad go away, or at least bury it under a lot of snow. I didn't realize our definitions of the word "snow" were different.

"Anyway, the long weekend was an attempt to woo me, to pretend nothing had changed, and I found out it hadn't. While we were there, Ray made an east-coast connection. This guy was a major player, a supplier with lots of money and power backing him. The guy had a real presence. He was the one everyone in the room noticed, the big dog. Didn't matter if you liked him or not. You noticed him.

"I hated him and Ray loved him. Watching the two of them together was like sitting in on someone else's first date, when one person is trying harder to make a good impression. Leo threw him a bone, told Ray he would be in touch. He gave Ray a little present before he left. 'Good stuff,' he said. Ray was in heaven. I was somewhere else.

"I'm OK for now, but, my optic nerve isn't quite right. Of course there isn't any official connection, but a friend of mine who's a nurse said it was quite possible. I just know. There isn't any other explanation. My eyes aren't the same. Something is different, but I can't quite name it. I don't know if they'll get worse, but I guess everything gets worse if we wait long enough."

"Does he know?"

"No. And I'm not going to tell him," she said. "My parents can get me the best

care. My dad's cousin is an ophthalmologist. He doesn't know, no one in my family knows, but when the time is right, I'll call."

"I'm sure there's a lot they can do now," I said, trying to find hope in the sound of my voice.

"Yeah, I guess so," she said. "Anyway, the desert relaxes me, I find the emptiness almost spiritual. And there's always a chance that nothing will change – with my eyes, I mean. If Ray knew about any of this, it would tear him up," she said. "He would probably kill himself."

I believed her.

I don't remember who left the table first, but we didn't stay much longer. I saw a guy walk on his hands back by the bathrooms. Rudy told me later that he does that in bars to win bets. On the way out the door, I asked Rudy about the football game with LeeAnn.

"It wasn't me, honey," he said. "She must be confusing me with someone else."

THE TRAIN RIDE

WANITA MARIE HUMPHREY

I kept looking for my brother, Jan, but I couldn't see him. The matron from the Children's Aid Society had said she would try to get us on the same train, but we had been separated when it was time to get on the bus to go to the station. I kept swallowing hard so that the lump in my throat would not cause me to start crying.

One of the chaperones was counting out loud so I knew there were thirty-seven of us. Thirty-seven wasn't so many. I should be able to find Jan. But I didn't, and when we were put on the train and assigned seats, I could see that he was not here.

I squeezed my eyes tight as the train slowly started to chug its way out of the station. The clacking of the wheels was a sound that took me farther from New York City. Farther from my neighborhood and the Polish people I had grown up with. Mama and Papa had both died of the fever and we had no other relatives. While the neighbors were kind, they were all too poor to take in two more children. We lived on the streets and slept in doorways. We were always hungry but sometimes could get a bit of money by blacking shoes or selling newspapers. So many like us became beggars. We did not like to beg, but sometimes... until one day, a gruff man made us go with him and that is how we had come to the Children's Aid Society.

The people from the Society gave us food, new clothes, and a place to sleep. They said that we would be sent to families who lived on farms. We would have good homes and plenty to eat. But Jan and I thought we would go together.

I couldn't keep the tears from sliding from my closed eyes as I thought about my brother who was two years younger. He was strong and brave for eight years old; there was nothing I could do but tell myself that he would be on another train, that he would have a good family and be happy. And maybe, just maybe, someday we could find each other.

Miss Elizabeth, one of the chaperones, told us that we were going to Illinois to live with German families on farms. I did not know much about farms—just that there were animals and growing crops. Would any of the customs be the same? In New York, there were people from so many places, that just a block or two away could seem like a different country. I took the knotted string from my pocket and began saying the rosary. I noticed one of the chaperones, a thin-faced man, giving me a hard look so I put it back in my pocket. Would I be allowed to pray the rosary in my new home?

The train was grinding to a slow stop. We were allowed to get off —to get fresh air and exercise, we were told. One of the chaperones was holding up some sort of sign and some people who had been waiting at the station came up to him. They talked for a few minutes and I saw them point to Jakub. He was a strong boy of about twelve years. The man holding the sign called Jakub over and said something to him. Jakub walked away with the people. This happened at more stops and there were fewer and fewer of us on the train.

I was starting to fall asleep when some of the others began shouting. I sat up quickly and saw that many of them had their noses pressed to the windows.

"Look! Look! Apples!" Indeed, stretching for what seemed miles there were trees with the bright red fruit. Perhaps there would be trees like these where we were going.

There was a large gathering of people at our last stop. My heart took turns almost stopping, but then beating so hard that I thought it might pop right out of my chest. When Miss Elizabeth pointed to me, I kept my eyes downcast as I walked toward her. There was a man and a woman. The man was saying something about taking me to my new home. He looked serious, but not unkind. The pretty woman smiled and reached out and put her hand on my shoulder. And then, from behind the man came a beautiful brown dog that sniffed at me and wagged his tail.

For the first time in a long time, I didn't feel so frightened. I think this new home is going to be a good place. If only Jan was here.

AUTHOR'S NOTE

In this time before social services or a foster care system, a minister, Charles Loring, founded the Children's Aid Society to address the plight of orphaned or abandoned children in New York City. Between 1854 and 1929, as many as 200,000 children were placed on trains and sent to farms in the west. This removed the children from the poverty of the city and provided labor for the farms. Many children rode to better lives, but others did not. Some were destined for pre-determined families, but a greater number were chosen at the train stops.

BLOWING BUBBLES

VIRGINIA LEE

The water has always called to me. Being in the ocean and becoming part of a different world has entranced me since I was too young to learn to scuba dive. I'd always planned on learning but life interfered and time passed. Twenty years later, I'm in Aruba walking down a sandy beach toward the water's edge, squinting in the bright sunlight and trying not to hunch over due to the steel scuba tank strapped to my back, ready to enter the ocean for my first open water scuba dive.

The rolling surf breaking and crashing on the beach sounds the same as every other tropical trip, but it's not. Today, when I enter, I won't have to stop once it reaches my head, I can keep going and remain under the waves. I'll have an air tank with me and will join this watery world.

Today will also be my first time in the open ocean where wild creatures great and small claim this as their domain, outside the safe confines of a twelve-foot-deep concrete pool. I'll be a visitor in this realm and I can't wait.

My instructor, Dario, turns toward me, standing effortlessly with the steel tank on his back like it was nothing more than an empty backpack. "Ready for this?"

I nod.

"Great, we'll do a few skills before going to deeper water."

I've waited years for this moment and ignore the butterflies skittering around my insides. My gaze goes toward the horizon—where the blues of the ocean and sky meld—water as far as I can see, no walls to swim to in a moment of panic.

"I'm ready," I say, with more confidence than I feel. My scuba skills are well honed. I'd done so many in the pool. But now I was in the ocean. Saltwater would sting my eyes, chlorine didn't. I was afraid my mask would flood, filling with saltwater, temporarily blinding me and causing me to end my dive by bolting recklessly to the surface. I didn't want my dream ruined.

"Let's go blow bubbles," Dario said, lowering his mask over his eyes and sinking into the surf.

A mixture of emotions fills me—excitement, fear and anxiety—we weren't jumping into the middle of a bottomless ocean but would be descending gradually, following the sloping shore towards the reef. Logically, I knew the beach and shallower water wouldn't be that far away, but being in a body of water that wasn't contained within concrete walls was different, both mentally and realistically. I had no idea how I would react. Would it bother me knowing the surface and the air I needed to breathe to stay alive would be far away? I sure hoped not. I hadn't come this far to fail.

Dario looked at me. I could see the question in his brown eyes. "You sure you're ready for this?"

"Yes," I said a bit louder than I meant to, maybe to help convince my worried inner voice. I adjusted my face mask, determined to succeed. Once we'd reached chest height, the water eased the weight of the tank on my back and I felt freer.

"Stop here and we'll put our fins on," Dario said, bending to pull his own fins over his feet.

I copied him, now realizing why we waited. The long fins would have made walking into the breaking surf difficult, with the tips catching the waves and probably making me fall. I tested the straps; my fins were secure. No chance of them falling off during the dive and making me look foolish.

Once we had reached shoulder height water, we stopped. "Let's do your drills and then swim down to the reef," Dario said, his white teeth flashing, as he smiled at me. His calmness rubbed off, giving me courage.

It was time.

I placed the regulator in my mouth and slipped under the surface, letting the rhythmic sounds of my breathing soothe me. My body relaxed. I hadn't realized how tense I'd been; the unknown of the open ocean had frightened me more than I realized,

I watched Dario as he signaled each skill. I could find my regulator if it came out of my mouth. I could replace my buoyancy compensator vest if I ever needed to, and lastly, I successfully cleared my mask and my eyes did not sting from the salt water.

A large grin, crinkling eyes and the OK signal from Dario meant I'd passed. We could finally go deeper. He motioned forward with his hand and headed down the sloping seabed.

The visibility had been murky due to the sand constantly being stirred up by the incoming and outgoing tide, but the deeper we swam the clearer the water became and a new world opened up. Beams of sunlight angled thru the water, dancing like spotlights on the bottom. Below me a barnacle-encrusted conch, with it distinctive conical spiral shaped shell, created a furrow in the sandy flat, only its antenna and front legs visible as it went on its slow march.

Colorful fish darted away as we approached – bright purple/ blue damselfish with yellow bellies and tail fins; angelfish that look like living works of art with their bold patterns, iridescent blue bodies and a crown shaped pattern on its head, and a few iconic orange and white striped clownfish – now forever known as Nemo.

What did these small creatures think of us? Large, unwieldy things noisily breathing through a tube and then exhaling streams of bubbles.

Dario turned toward me, met my gaze and signaled OK, waiting for me to return the sign before going any deeper. Exhilaration coursed through me; I returned his signal with my own OK. He grinned, nodded and swam slowly next to me as we kept descending, following the sea floor.

I pulled my gauges forward and checked our depth and the amount of air in my tank. We were at 25 feet and my air gauge read almost full. That made me happy because I remembered learning that nervous people can suck more air and quickly empty their tanks. I'd always had

plenty of air in the pool sessions and had hoped that would carry over into my ocean dives, and it did. Another worry I could cross of my list.

My eyes grew round and I grinned. The colors were all so brilliant, so bold and bright. All around me were gorgeous, healthy corals. Stony tan colored staghorn coral reached upward, its forked branches resembling antlers. Green mounds of mountainous star coral created boulder shapes along the base of the reef. Orange and red soft flower coral with its cup-shaped polyps amazed me. Purple veined sea fans gracefully waved back and forth in the current, fish weaving in and out. Several schools of tiny juvenile fish grouped together, like a fish nursery, skittering for the safety of the openings in the coral when bigger fish came to close. Towards the deeper blue water, a school of barracuda swam by, their silvery torpedo shaped bodies quite distinctive. They flashed in the sunlight as they swam through the rays penetrating the water.

Life surrounded us, and I was in the midst of it. This time I wasn't watching a nature documentary, I was immersed in one.

We hovered above an opening in the coral and watched as a bright green moray eel slid in and out of its hiding spot, mouth gaping, sharp teeth waiting to snag lunch. Its black eyes glanced at us and it was hard not to back away. I knew the eel wouldn't zip out and attack, but it's hard to keep logical thoughts in your mind when you're actually in that situation and not reading about it from the comfort of your living room.

I heard tapping and looked toward my instructor. Dario banged his steel tank with a metal carabiner. He motioned toward an outcropping in the reef and swam closer to it. I followed him and when I saw what he was pointing at, my heart thudded, either from excitement or fear, I wasn't sure.

Under the ledge, no more than ten feet, were sharks. I would later find out they were nurse sharks, but seeing two sharks staring back at you in the open ocean is a little unsettling. Alarmed, I looked at Dario wondering why he wasn't retreating. He signaled it was OK, but I didn't quite believe that, but if he thought it was all right to stay, I wasn't about to leave him to scurry to the surface and the relative safety of shallower water.

I had never been this close to sharks before and it was thrilling, after I got over my fear of thinking they were going to launch themselves at us and eat us. Their bodies blended perfectly with the sand, a mixture of brown, white and tan Their gills opened and closed with their breaths as they absorbed oxygen from the water flowing through them. They appeared to be resting calmly on the bottom. Little barbels hung from their mouths, like catfish Their lidless eyes stared calmly at us. After a few second, but what seemed much longer, the sharks lost interest in us and looked away, wriggling their bodies further under the coral ledge.

Dario motioned for us to continue. We watched iridescent neon parrot fish with their bird-like beaks dive toward the coral, take a bite and then back away, chewing their snack. The parrotfish repeated this dance several times and then what was left of the coral came out the other end as sand.

I was so enthralled with the underwater life, that when Dario signaled me to check my gauges, the reading surprised me. We had descended to 70 feet - deeper than I had thought. I

glanced upward and could still see the undulating surface. I realized then how deceptive depth can be, especially in clear water with good visibility. Luckily, I still had half a tank of air which reassured me.

As much as I wanted to linger and remain in the fishy world, Dario pointed his thumb upward, signaling it was time to ascend and finish the dive. I nodded and swam along next to him as we followed the rising sea floor towards the beach. As we ascended, the coral growths became fewer until the bottom became mainly sand broken up by patches of greenish-brown sea grass. We stopped when we reached 15 feet, to hover for three minutes. It was necessary to allow our bodies time to expel the built-up gas in our blood streams from breathing compressed air.

The forty minutes underwater had seemed like five. It went by too quickly. I would've stayed down there all day if possible. When we reached waist deep water and stood up, I pulled off my mask, grinning from ear to ear.

Dario laughed. "I don't need to ask what you thought of your first ocean dive. I can see your enjoyment in your face."

"It was better than I imagined. I can hardly believe I wanted so long to get certified. I can't wait to get back under the waves and blow bubbles."

THE ANIMATED CAROUSEL

VIRGINIA LEE

When the carnival came to town, the carnies stopped at the edge, between habited and uninhabited land, or so they thought. They stopped where the houses ended, where the fields and brambles grew in a wild tangle. In a small strip, they set up their tents, the rides, the games-of-chance, and most importantly, the carousel, for every carnival has a carousel.

The carnies scurried, unloading every ride and booth before the black of night fell. They wanted to be safely in their campers, doors locked, tucked in, away from the unsettling sense of their latest location. Although the barren ground looked perfect—wide and flat—something seemed off. No birds sang their evening songs; the air smelled different – almost too sweet but with an undertone bordering on rot.

The brightly painted carousel with a red and white striped canopy rising high from a gleaming steel center pole was placed at the carnival's entrance, away from the other rides on the midway. Carved horses, rabbits, giraffes, and lions waited, captured in position, either rising or falling. Care had been taken when creating the carousel creatures; upon first glance they appeared real; eyes glistened, the gaping lion's mouth seemed to drip with saliva and the rabbit's wide dark eyes reflected fear. Every animal struck an action pose—running, jumping, or rearing—none appeared to be merely standing.

Horses of every color were waiting, waiting for a child to come ride them. Near the front stood a white stallion, neck arched, flaring nostrils rimmed in red, blue-black mane flying in an invisible wind. Faintly, near the base of the mane, the white paint was marred by a faint reddish-brown smear. The stallion's front legs reached forward as if to strike an invisible enemy, while its rear legs were drawn toward its body, ready to launch the horse airborne.

An ornately decorated saddle sat on its back, the green saddle pad beneath trimmed with gold braiding and dripping rubies, sapphires, and emeralds. The horse's tail arched and then streamed out behind like a plume of darkest smoke. A brilliant red and green bridle, trimmed with gold hearts etched into the cheek pieces, matched the breast plate with blue tassels slanting backwards, making it seem like the horse was racing toward a destiny known only to it.

But in the middle of every animal, a pole ran through their bodies. A pole connecting them to the steel ring that moved in clockwise circles every time the carousel turned on. A wide brass pole always reminding them that they have no choice. Their life, their movement, is at the mercy of the pole. When it goes up, so does the animal and when it goes down, the animal must follow. Choice does not exist on the carousel.

During the black of the night, when the carnies had pulled the covers over their heads, shut their blinds against the unknown, something stirred, something that sensed life where there had been none for many long years. Above it, in the pale light of the moon, waited the carousel.

The ground where the carnival had been placed was not empty—it was barren for a reason and that reason found hope. It knew something was up there, something that called out with the softest of sounds. From the darkest of places, hope sparked from what had been left of the remnants of a shattered curse. Awoken from a troubled slumber, the elemental entity gathered strength from the carnival above, drawing to it what had been denied for so long.

From deep in the ground, the entity rose upward in an inky plume, seeking out the cracks where the carnies had hammered in the stakes, anchoring the rides, and the tents. These very

holes were all it needed. Nothing had scored this land in recent memory; the townsfolk did not remember why this section of land remained undeveloped. But those below do not mark time the same. Two hundred years or two days were the same.

The entity rose, seeking. The desire to no longer be a shapeless being pulsated through the entity, propelling it to find the host.

A silvery smoke wafted over the ground, snaking along silently, like a molten river. It moved with an invisible breeze, twining itself around the ropes holding up the big top and then sliding off as if finding them unsuitable. Quickly it slithered down to the ground and continued on, still searching.

Near the staked tent, the carousel sat still and quiet, all the animals resting, or so it seemed. The white stallion, closest to the seeking plume, moved just the tiniest bit. If a carnie had chosen to look out his window, it might have seemed his eyes had played a trick.

But it was not an illusion. The stallion's ears—pinned back toward the rippling mane caught in a timeless semblance of motion—flicked. The black eye, painted to face forward, to its destiny, rolled sideways just a bit. The flaring, red-lined nostrils, expanded as if taking a long-awaited breath.

Sensing its desire, the ghostly plume expanded and then raced toward the white horse with the black and blue mane. Like fog on a river, it rose and surrounded the stallion. Pouring itself through the opening in the red-lined nostrils, the open mouth with pink tongue and gleaming teeth chomping at the silver bit, and the hole created by the brass pole.

The second the entity touched it; the horse became aware. Like blood infusing the painted veins and muscles, the horse knew it existed, knew it had another purpose. The horse was no longer an object doomed to go around in circles for eternity. The stallion savored the delicious feeling of the entity pouring its life into the once inanimate body. Everywhere it touched, the horse vibrated and radiated, greedily sucking energy.

"Give me life," the stallion whispered.

At first, the plume filled a hollow body but the longer it swirled inside the horse, the more changes took place. A once empty shell began to grow. From a tiny spark, life burst into glorious existence. A creature of blood and bones grew. A beating heart formed, forcing life to limbs aching to move, to run. Blood pumped and needed a place to live; veins and arteries formed, bones, muscles and also a brain.

A brain that demanded release, release from the imprisoning pole binding the stallion to the carousel. One thought sounded loudest. Freedom. Freedom from the prison that had held it for countless years, ever since its creator had infused the essence of life in the carving with the blood from a living horse, knowing, hoping, one day the door would open and the horse would come alive. The red-brown handprint under the mane pulsated, finally fulfilling its destiny.

The stallion had awareness. It let out a long, loud neigh, tossing its head, the once still blue/black mane now rippled with movement. Legs that were frozen in place now flexed and kicked the metal floor, the sound reverberating.

But the stallion still could not leave. The pole spearing the body kept it in place. The painted black eyes now glowed red. The snort of breath from the nostrils were like two streams of steam. The horse gathered its leg underneath preparing to jump but when it placed its hooves down, the body did not move.

Anger filled the horse. The stallion wanted, needed, only one thing, freedom. It had been kept captive for too long.

Gathering strength, the horse gave a mighty push, breaking away from the hated pole impaling its perfect body. The pole snapped as the horse tore away, opening a large gash. Bright red blood ran down the horse's sides, staining the saddle and pooling in the shadow of where the horse once stood. Bits of flesh and hair remained on the broken pole which now had streaks of blood.

The pole left wide open gashes in the horse's back and belly. Torn flesh hung from the belly, dripping with blood. Muscles bunched and strained as the horse gathered its legs underneath and pushed off, away from the carousel, finally free. As the stallion galloped into the night, the jagged flesh reached together, fusing, repairing the ragged wounds.

Through the gaping holes, the entity swirled out, leaving some of its essence in the horse and quickly dividing. More inanimate creatures waited, the only beings it had the capability to possess. Being freed from the dark, dank earth had given the entity power, power to divide and grow. It sought out the other carousel creatures, pouring life-giving essence into them.

The sound of screaming animals, groaning and cracking metal ripped the night. The dark entity filled each one with supernatural life and in turn they ripped away from the carousel, fleeing into the dark night. When the carnies awoke in the morning and opened their doors, all that was left of the carousel were shattered poles, broken limbs and pools of dried blood.

MOUNT TOM

ROD MCHUGH

When the morning sun crested the White Mountains, the snow-capped peak of Mt. Tom glistened in the sunlight. For millennia, this pyramidic structure of volcanic rock and time has stood sentinel over the comings and goings of the Valley below.

Once home to Native Americans, cattle ranchers, and farmers, this formerly arable land on the eastern side of the Sierras became an oasis for outdoor enthusiasts who traveled the length and breadth of Highway 395 to experience nature in the rough.

For many, the jumping off point was Bishop, California; a small town nestled between the Whites and the Sierras at the northern edge of the high desert valley named for Richard Owens, one of Fremont's guides. Besides the valley, the river that flows through it bears his name, as does the dry lake into which it once emptied. And although the former still makes its contribution to the valley, the latter lost its glory when Mr. Mulholland diverted its waters to the burgeoning L. A. Basin via an intricate system of canals in 1913. Incited by this outrageous action the residents of the Valley became embroiled in a water–rights dispute with the City of Los Angeles that continues to this day.

Now if this story seems familiar, perhaps the reader has seen the film, *Chinatown*, in which the historic struggle served as backdrop to the corruption and chicanery of L. A. politics in the 1930s. In contrast, our present tale views the Valley through the eyes of a returning veteran clinging to Post-War promises and the hope of securing a new life.

AFTER BEING DISCHARGED from the Army in the Autumn of '45, I stuck around Europe for a while. When I finally returned to Southern California, my Aunt Jane, an energetic, ninety-year-old, invited me to join her on a fishing trip above Bishop.

While driving back to her cabin following an incredible day of fishing on Lake Sabrina, the ol' girl fell silent. By the time I was able to pull over, she was gone. From that minute on, everything became a blur.

On Tuesday, her body was cremated; her will was read on Friday, and to my astonishment, she had bequeathed me all her worldly assets, including the cabin on Bishop Creek. To say I was shocked is putting it mildly; to say I was grateful, hardly covers the half of it. A month later, having settled my accounts in Long Beach, I returned to the place where I had spent the happiest days of my youth.

When I pulled up to the cabin that afternoon, a strange melancholia shrouded me. Aunt Jane wasn't standing on the porch shouting, "Hurry up and get that car unpacked, you sorry excuse for a boy! We got fishin' to do!" I sat motionlessly, reflecting on all the happiness I had known there and how in the days ahead I'd have plenty of time to fish but no Jane to enjoy it with.

The rat-ta-tat-tat sound of a woodpecker disturbed the solemnity of the moment, bringing me back to reality.

Key in hand, I climbed out of the green '42 Ford pick-up, grabbed my grip from the truck bed, leaving the trunk for later, and headed to the porch.

Unlocking the front door, I swung it open and crossed the threshold only to be stopped in my tracks by a well-placed southpaw of odor; its smell was neither bitter like vinegar, nor aggressive like turpentine. On the contrary, it was delicate, refined...familiar.

In fact, it reminded me of Aunt Jane standing before her bureau in full regalia, spritzer in hand, "fitzing" her favorite perfume in the air, then gliding through the mist----Over the years, that mixture of wild-flowers and sandalwood must have absorbed itself into the cushions, curtains, and furnishings of the old place.

The experience reminded me of something I'd read about concerning the passing of loved ones. The author argued that the deceased often leave little remembrances behind lest we forget them too soon.

Closing the door, I placed the suitcase on the floor and sauntered over to her chair---I took a seat. It was an old winged-back rocker upholstered in forest green wool with a faint floral pattern etched into its fabric. White doilies were pinned on the arms and the back where the head might rest. Its twin graced the flip side of a mahogany table upon which a shaded brass lamp stood.

Just opposite the chairs set a sofa covered in like material and possessing its own set of doilies. Matching end tables performed their duties like parentheses in a well-written sentence, while shaded lamps waited patiently to cast light upon this tiny world which had once known much happiness.

Separating the "living room" from the kitchen was an oak dining table with six straight-back chairs, all hand-carved by my Uncle Lee.

The walls of the great room were decorated with framed paintings by local artists and a montage of black and white photographs taken by my cousin from Buena Park. Each picture was carefully displayed either in groupings or singularly, depending on the emotion my aunt wished them to convey.

On the north wall, a large fireplace constructed of gray river rock stood ready to keep the tenants warm. The two bedrooms on the south-side of the cabin enjoyed the functionality of Ben Frank stoves.

On either side of the front door, large, thick-paned picture windows filled the appropriate spaces; thick, wool drapes could be drawn to bar the cold. Smaller windows were centered on the walls of each bedroom and the kitchen. Aunt Jane had left nothing to chance; everything necessary for one's comfort was there…everything but her laughter.

Then unexpectedly, the tears I had avoided since her demise rallied *en masse*. And although I tried my damnedest, I couldn't do a thing to stop them; they were determined to have their way…and so I sat obligingly in her chair until they were fully spent.

In the meantime, the sun hesitantly withdrew its light from the room as it inched its way behind the western rim of the peaks. When, at last, the darkness inside surpassed that which stood sentry outside, I lighted a lamp.

Ticking away the remains of the day was an old grandfather Clock standing in the corner of the room. Aunt Jane's aromatic presence comforted me. After an hour or so, the rhythmic caresses of the pendulum coaxed my eyes to close.

DESPITE MY MONTHLY pension covering my essentials adequately, I decided to subsidize my income by performing odd jobs for my neighbors. Before long the news of my craftsmanship spread from one coffee shop to another. By the fifth month, my reputation for being a "first-rate fixer" kept me working steadily.

Initially, my little enterprise serviced Bishop alone. But by mid-Summer the human telegraph praised my abilities as far as the County Seat. By the following Spring, my phone number had travelled the full circuit of the Valley via residents who stopped at Schat's Bakery in Lone Pine on their way to and from the Southland.

Never being one who needs more than the basics to survive, I had gotten on well that first winter. By the following one, I felt thoroughly acclimated to my new World…and once again, I thanked Destiny for Aunt Jane's gracious gift that made it possible for me to live in a place where I'd never been happier.

PRIOR TO RECEIVING Uncle Sam's invitation to fight Fascism in Europe, I had been an English major at Long Beach Community College. But when War was declared, I covered my typewriter and put scholarship on hold.

When the War ended in '45, I stuck around Europe for a while. Finally returning to the States in the Autumn of '46, I determined to complete my Associates. To graduate with honors, I wrote a thesis on the *Psychology of War*. After all that, however, my degree sat idle... until one afternoon in late Summer, 1949.

I was repairing a picket fence in Big Pine, when the thought occurred to me as I hammered the last nail into the last slat of what would be my last fence, that I ought to put my education to work. The question was, "how?"

When I got home that evening, I sat on the porch smoking my pipe while mulling over what one could do with an English degree. The tobacco had been spent for some time when the idea hit me: I'd become a newspaper reporter.

So tucking my new ambition in my breast pocket, I drove down the hill next morning to see Rex Foley, the editor of the Bishop Gazette, concerning the possibility of his hiring me. While he was chewing on the idea, I spelled out my thoughts on the matter.

I had it figured to write weekly articles on everything from Mule Days (our annual Fair) to the Ladies' Auxiliary Meetings, which met once a month in the VFW Hall, as did the VFW members themselves.

Now these latter meetings had traditionally been open to men only, until Miss Abigail Murphy insisted upon joining them. Surprisingly, no one dared raise an objection because of her gender. She had, after all, served meritoriously as an Army nurse in the Philippines...*and* miraculously survived an internment camp.

Well, it didn't take me long to sell Foley on the idea. He did, however, say that he'd been toying with the same idea himself. I smiled and nodded, and then reported to work the following Monday morning.

My articles highlighted community events like our Rodeo in the summer, and the High School's sports program throughout the school year. These activities brought crowds of varying sizes to town, depending upon the activity and their distance from Bishop.

But the stories I enjoyed writing the most were the ones focused on the outdoor activities which characterized life on the eastern side of the Sierras. I decided to incorporate residents of the Valley into them, thus making the articles more personal to our immediate population. To accomplish this, I rustled up those locals who had fished our waterways or climbed the varying peaks in the region, including Mt. Whitney; anything that captured the interests of outdoor enthusiasts.

During my fourth year on the job, Ed Moran, the assistant editor of the Fresno Bee, passed through Bishop on his way to his brother Jed's. He lived outside of town near Laws, and a great sports enthusiast.

While strolling around town, Ed stopped in the Bishop Café for a cup of coffee. Plopping down in one of the booths, he happened on a discarded Gazette. He turned to the editorial page and read several letters to the Editor concerning one of my articles on backpacking above Lone Pine. He asked a few customers about "this chap" who had written the referenced article.

Well, whatever they told him, Moran liked it enough to stop by our office the following day to discuss the possibility of publishing my articles in The Bee. By five o'clock, the three of us came to an agreement. The stories would be published in both papers but given a spin to appeal to the specific audience.

Once my stories were published in the San Joaquin Valley, the plan cross pollenated. First with the Modesto Bee and then the Sacramento Bee a month later.

Strange as it may seem, we were inundated with questions from the readers. Mr. Foley wasn't surprised at all; in fact, he was pleased. He solved the issue by assigning two part-time employees to combine the questions by topic, thereby condensing the answers. The strategy proved effective.

A few months later, while I was sitting on the porch smoking my pipe, I looked up at the stars and thanked Aunt Jane once again for her gracious gift. At that very moment, a shooting star streaked across the sky. I believe to this day it was her saying, *"Your welcome."*

IF THIS BE HEAVEN.....

FRANK MONTAGNINO

The paperwork had been completed and Wally had filled out all the blanks. The interview had gone pretty well, he thought, although he was a little disappointed that St. Peter himself hadn't been there to conduct it. Disappointed, but not surprised, he admitted. Wally had never put much stock in the old tale of St. Peter standing at the Pearly Gates and singlehandedly reviewing each applicant's life history, then deciding which souls were worthy of admittance. He recalled Groucho Marx' beautiful line about "not wanting to be a part of any club that would have him as a member," but as soon as the line went through his head he looked around sheepishly as though up here everyone could read his thoughts. Taken in this context Groucho's line suddenly became blasphemous.

No, he mused, the real process of getting into heaven was totally different than he'd been led to expect. People still alive would be astonished at the businesslike atmosphere. It was very much like applying for a white-collar position in the earthly job market - sterile and stressful, especially given the alternative. Thinking of that fiery alternative, Wally felt extremely grateful that he had received the stamp of approval and had been ushered through a spectacular gateway to the kingdom of heaven.

"There he is!"

Wally turned to locate the source of the voice. He almost broke into tears when he saw his mother and father waiting to greet him. They looked good - healthy and happy and very glad to see him.

After a long, heartfelt hug, maybe the best, warmest, most welcoming embrace he'd ever experienced, Wally held his mom at arm's length. She looked wonderful, but different, somehow. Her features seemed to be liquid, constantly changing. At first, she looked the same as the last time he'd seen her in the hospital with thinning grey hair and a stoutish frame that on anyone other than your mother you'd classify as fat. An instant later, her face looked like it did when he was ten or eleven, with dark brown hair upswept into a kind of tube shape that made almost a complete circle around her head. It must have been the style of the day, he mused. Her body changed too into the younger, slimmer version of herself that he remembered from long ago.

Wally looked at his dad to see if the same thing was happening to him. It was. Whereas at first glance his dad looked just like he did in his later years, in the next instant he was a much younger version of himself, sporting the neat mustache he'd worn occasionally before and after he went into the Army during WW II.

Grandma and Grandpa looked great too although Wally wasn't quite sure how they arrived on the scene. Just materialized, he surmised. As he remembered from years ago, he had to bend low to hug Grandma who at full height barely came up to his chest. Grandpa's kiss, full on the lips as always, featured the same bristly scrape of his handlebar mustache and the faint aroma of his stinky black crook cigars. Although he was almost euphoric with delight at seeing his beloved relatives again, Wally couldn't help noticing that unlike his parents, Grandma and Grandpa's features didn't change. Wally reasoned that he'd only known them as older people so that's the way he'd continue to see them. He felt confident, however that his dad would see them as both old and young and everything in between.

A sudden and completely unrelated thought came to Wally and he looked down toward his feet. The clouds swirled around his shoes - probably a product of all the movies he'd seen. But he was relieved that he couldn't see through the clouds. Couldn't see Earth and therefore couldn't see what people still alive were doing. He felt immensely glad of that because when he was alive, he had always feared that mom, in heaven, might be able to look down and see him at his worst, most intimate, most embarrassing moments.

Wally's next surprise came when the group left the entry portal. There was no transportation system. One instant Wally would be with a crowd of old friends and family and the next he'd be sitting in a ballpark, or on the banks of a stream, or in a museum, or some other pleasant location. And he hadn't had to walk or drive to get from one place to another. In fact, he didn't even have to wish he were somewhere else. He was transported instantly from one location to another and without any sensation of movement. It was as though someone had invented a method of transportation that was more advanced even than mind-travel. There wasn't any thinking involved. It just happened. One moment he'd be in Grandma and Grandpa's old place in Brooklyn and the next he'd be seated on the ancient stones outside the Colosseum in Rome. And of course, if he ever wanted to be somewhere else, somewhere special, it just happened. That was neat.

One disappointment to this new way of transportation was that he didn't ever fly. In life Wally had always had the urge to fly. Not fly in planes of course, although he liked that too, but to fly by himself like a bird. He'd dreamed countless times about being able to will himself to slowly rise and soar into the sky. He'd always thought that flying like that would be one of the rewards of getting into heaven. And now that he was here, he was a little disappointed that flying wasn't even necessary.

Food didn't seem to be a big thing in heaven either. Wally quickly found there didn't seem to be set times for meals. Of course, if he wanted something to eat, bam, there it was. And if he wanted to experience an old family dinner - like the Sunday get-togethers at grandma's house - bang, there he was with all the uncles, aunts, and cousins, everybody laughing and talking over one another. And there'd come Uncle Mike with the pastries from Lindy's - the cheesecake, cannoli and especially the sfogliatelli. In some ways, Wally thought, Heaven was an extension of his earthly dreams and memories.

But an important difference, he discovered was that for any occasion or event you didn't have to *get there*. Wally didn't have to go through the process of getting dressed and getting in the car and going up the steps and all that. Scenes just faded into one another, like in a movie. If he wanted to see someone or be with them, he didn't have to call up and make arrangements, they simply appeared. And not at the door either, they were just *there* - on the chair next to him or across the kitchen table. And when they left, they didn't come up to him and say, "we're going now, we had a great time," and go out the door. They just disappeared. And they didn't just dissolve or fade away. They were just gone.

The whole concept of housing was delightfully puzzling in heaven. There didn't seem to be houses unless one was necessary to fulfill whatever scenario Wally was currently experiencing. Time was immaterial in heaven. Lord knows you weren't going anywhere. And since there were no time constraints there was no need to go home after a hard day of work. Thus, there was no need of homes. Of course, there was no work, either. Wally assumed that getting rid of work had been a top priority. What's more, you could hardly be expected to put in a day's work if there were no days. Instead of days there were 'events.' Things happened to Wally at his own desire; in an endless segue of events. These sequences of events were never terminated by sunrises or sunsets unless, of course, Wally wanted to enjoy a sunrise or sunset. In that case, one would occur even at high noon. Except that there was no noon.

In life, Wally had always enjoyed playing golf, so he was delighted to learn that in heaven he could play any golf course at any time. No tee times required, either. He would arrive right at the first tee. And he knew this was remarkable because there were jillions of other golfers in heaven enjoying the same privilege at the same time. Yet the courses were never crowded. As for the game itself, on occasion Wally could execute shots he could never duplicate on earth. Fantastically long, straight-as-a-string drives and high, arching iron shots that came down just past the pin and spun back toward the hole just like the top professionals used to do on TV. Yet he didn't automatically set new course records every time he played. Although his scores were better than on earth, they weren't *that much* better. Even in heaven the game remained deliciously complex and challenging. In truth, he realized, he wouldn't have had it any other way.

All in all, Wally thought, Heaven was a pretty good place. There were no murders or atrocities. There weren't even any minor irritations. There were no aches and pains and thus no need for aspirin or medicine cabinets. There were no chores or jobs and thus no deadlines or stress. There was grass of course, beautiful rolling lawns and fairways, but Wally didn't have to mow or tend them. No one did except for those people who took great pleasure in it. There were no traffic snarls or fender benders because there were no cars. That in turn eliminated the need for car salespeople, insurance companies and agents. And of course, there were no lawyers. They weren't allowed admittance. Nor were career politicians.

Not long after Wally got to Heaven, indeed while he was still learning the ropes, he was summoned by a very polite and gracious woman for an admittance interview with the Lord. "We all get a chance to meet with the Lord," she explained. "Would you mind waiting? We're a little backed up."

Wally settled into a comfortable chair and idly leafed through a stack of magazines on the table next to him. They were all the latest editions of publications that actually interested him. There was *Golf Digest* and *Sports Illustrated* and *Car and Driver* and of course, *Reader's Digest*. There were no publications on child-rearing or religion or income tax preparation or Hollywood celebrities. Wally assumed those publications would have been on the table had someone else been sitting in his place. Still, something bothered him and he rose and strode back through the knee-high clouds to the reception desk.

"Excuse me," he said, "but I was just wondering why there are magazines in heaven? When I was on earth, it seemed as though the whole publishing industry was dying. I kind of expected magazines would have been replaced by smart phones or electronic tablets or something else up here."

"Oh no," she explained with a smile. "Those annoying electronic devices aren't permitted."

"Ahhh, I see," Wally nodded. "One other thing. Since there is no time element and no deadlines or appointments, why is it you're backed up and that I have to wait to see the Lord?"

The woman leaned forward and gestured for Wally to bend closer so she could whisper.

"She's in the ladies room."

A POSTCARD FOR THE LONELY

MARGARET SETTLE

She sat each day at her window silently watching the village in motion. She watched as workers left and returned from work. She watched children go to and from school. She watched the early morning and evening dog walkers. She watched trash pick-up and mail deliveries. On this day, a single postcard arrived. A picture of far-away tranquility. A note of happiness and adventure. Contentment and memories return. Who knew the power of a postcard?

AT LAST

SUSETTE V. SHREVE

He weighed the book in his right hand, it felt lighter than the last piece he'd authored. As an unpublished manuscript it had been a hope, a dream. In the end, it just fizzled out. He'd lost interest. It'd been thrown into the old cabinet made of applewood his father had left him. It was where all his writings went to die. At least that's what he'd told himself. But he, Jeffery Jeffson, wasn't a quitter this time and so he plugged on and on never giving up even when it seemed everyone around him had said, stop. Thumbing through the pages the print size seemed sufficient enough. The larger the text the better, that and white space. This was going to be his debut, the first of many notable novels. Placing his book back on a shelf along with all the other published authors, Jeffery smiled, he had arrived at last

THE CHRISTMAS ANGEL

BILLIE HOLLADAY SKELLEY

Christmas was less than a month away, but in 1862, the holiday held little promise of merriment. Snow covered Washington, D. C., and to Clarissa Harlowe Barton the whole world seemed cold, even the White House. Shivering in her best dress and thickest shawl, she watched as President Lincoln talked with the newly-appointed commander of the Union Army of the Potomac, Ambrose Burnside. From her vantage point, it didn't appear that General Burnside was excited about his new position, but before she could study the two men further, President Lincoln motioned for her to join them.

"Miss Barton, please allow me to introduce General Burnside. He seems anxious to make your acquaintance."

General Burnside bowed at the waist.

"Good evening, Miss Barton."

"It's a pleasure to meet you, General Burnside. Please call me Clara."

"I have a request to make of you, but I fear it may place you in danger."

"Please, just tell me, General Burnside."

"I need you to travel to a colonial mansion in Falmouth, Virginia. It's called Lacy House, and the home sits on a large plantation on the banks of the Rappahannock, opposite the city of Fredericksburg. I need you to establish a hospital in the place as quickly as possible."

"Thank you, General Burnside. I will depart right away."

"I have six wagons with supplies already prepared. There is a buggy waiting for you, and Cornelius Welles will accompany you as your driver."

"Thank you, General."

Wrapping her shawl tightly around her shoulders, Clara Barton left the White House. Outside snow continued to fall, but she found Cornelius, and he escorted her to the buggy. She was pleased to see he had provided several quilts for the journey. As soon as she was settled, they were on the road.

Their trip took several days, but Clara was in residence at Lacy House by the seventh of December. She recruited several assistants to help her, including May and Jeb Rainey who lived in Falmouth. They immediately went to work transforming the palatial home into a functional hospital. Working day and night, they set up beds, distributed blankets, prepared bandages, hauled water, and gathered food.

Although Lacy House was huge by normal living standards, Clara worried whether there would be enough room for the wounded soldiers. From what she could discern from snippets of overheard conversation, the Union was preparing for a huge battle, and General Burnside hoped to cut the Confederates off from their capital in Richmond. With so many troops assembling, Clara knew there would be many wounded.

On December the eleventh, Clara stood on the second-floor balcony of Lacy House watching thousands of Confederate troops assembling in Fredericksburg, on the other side of the Rappahannock River. As she watched, Union engineers began constructing a pontoon bridge across the wide, frigid Rappahannock, so their soldiers could cross the river. They had hardly begun, when Confederate snipers, barricaded in Fredericksburg's tall buildings, began firing on them. The engineers had to run for cover, and the bridge construction ceased. Suddenly, Clara heard the Union artillery, stationed near Lacy House, erupt. Federal guns began bombarding Fredericksburg to stop the snipers. Clara watched as a barrage of shells tore the town to pieces. Then, the Union engineers returned to finish their work on the bridge.

Transfixed for a minute by all the activity, Clara rose to action when she saw Union soldiers being carried toward Lacy House. Running down the stairs, she realized the Battle of Fredericksburg had officially begun.

By the time Clara reached the first floor, wounded men were already lying in the foyer of Lacy House. She immediately began staunching the flow of blood from their gunshot wounds, applying bandages, assessing the severity of injuries, and assigning beds. The remainder of the day went by in a blur as more and more wounded soldiers arrived. Because of the weather, Clara had to keep the fires in the fireplaces going constantly so the men stayed warm. She went from bed to bed carrying water to cleanse soldiers' wounds, and then she brought hot soup to those who were hungry.

As more and more wounded soldiers arrived, Clara worried whether they would have enough room, but she vowed not to turn anyone away.

The following day, a soldier arrived in the foyer of Lacy House, waving a folded piece of paper, and yelling for Miss Barton. Clara took the note and quickly read the message. It was from Dr. J. Clarence Cutter, a surgeon with the 21st Massachusetts, who was across the river on the battlefield. His message read: "Come to me. Your place is here."

Clara grabbed a warm cloak, a bag of medical supplies, and as much food and water as she could carry. Snow was falling as she left Lacy House and headed for the river. The bitter wind stung her face and hands. At the river's edge, she halted. Snipers were still shooting at those who tried to cross the river, and the recently constructed bridge did not look very stable.

Marshaling her courage, Clara stepped on the bridge and immediately felt alarmed. The bridge moved with each gust of wind. It swayed with each ripple of current. Her legs felt weak, and she didn't know if she could remain upright. Then, shots rang out. Bullets landed in the water right beside her. She was afraid to keep going, but then she remembered the wounded men waiting for her. Gathering her courage one more time, she started running, and soon found herself on the other side of the river.

Stepping off the bridge, a cannon shell dropped beside her and exploded. The impact knocked her to the ground and tore away part of her skirt. Quickly getting up, she asked the closest soldier to take her to Dr. Cutter.

The soldier brought her to where Dr. Cutter was working on the battlefield. He was surrounded by hundreds of bodies strewn in all directions.

"What is this place?" she asked.

"They're calling it the Slaughter Pen," Dr. Cutter answered. "Wave after wave of our soldiers try to advance, but there's a tremendous amount of rifle and artillery fire from the Confederates. They seem to have the high ground. Thousands have been killed, and we have a horrific number of wounded. Just start with those nearest, and do the best you can."

Clara began washing and bandaging the wounds of the soldiers closest to her. A fragment from an exploding shell had severed a soldier's artery, and she quickly applied a tourniquet. Most of the men were freezing in the frigid temperatures, and she did what she could to make them warm.

When Dr. Cutter called to her, she returned to his side and assisted him with amputations and the setting of broken limbs, as bullets flew over their heads. They dressed wounds and tried to stabilize as many men as they could.

When ambulance workers began to carry some of the severely wounded to a field hospital, Clara joined them. Doctors in the hospital were working feverishly, but the magnitude of the slaughter was difficult to grasp. So many had already succumbed, and so many others were lying in agony.

For the rest of that day, the entire night, and the next day, Clara tended to the fallen soldiers in the field hospital and throughout the decimated city. When the food and water she had brought with her was gone, she set up a soup kitchen. The temperature fell below freezing, and sometimes she wondered if she could keep moving. Her hands became so cold that she had difficulty getting her fingers to work, but she continued on.

When Dr. Cutter finally caught up with her again, he told her to return to Lacy House to rest.

Tired, hungry, and frostbitten, Clara made her way back across the river, but when she arrived at Lacy House, she was astonished to see how the stately home had been transformed. So many wounded soldiers now filled the house, she could hardly move around. All the beds were full. Soldiers were lying on the floor, in the hallways, and even on the stairs.

Clara tried to estimate how many soldiers were in her care and quickly realized it was over a thousand. Even with the fires in the fireplaces burning brightly, many soldiers complained of feeling cold. All their blankets were in use, so Clara asked her helpers to heat up bricks in the fireplaces. She told them to wrap the warm bricks in the soldiers' clothing and place them beside the men who were cold. She asked Jeb Rainey to bring in straw for those lying on the floor so they could at least rest a little more comfortably.

Although she was exhausted, Clara started washing wounds and bandaging injuries. She cared for all the soldiers in one room of the house, and then she moved on to another area.

Suddenly, more wounded arrived at the door of Lacy House, but these wounded men were Confederate soldiers. May Rainey began yelling at them to go away.

"Leave," May shouted. "We don't have enough food and bandages for our own soldiers, and there's certainly not enough for the enemy!"

Clara told May to stop shouting.

"Wounded soldiers are wounded soldiers," Clara said, "no matter what color their uniforms are."

"But Miss Barton we don't have any more room."

"I'll find the room."

Clara had the wounded Confederate soldiers brought inside, and she put them anywhere she could find an empty space. Some were placed on sofas, benches, shelves, under tables, and even on the top of cupboards. Others had to be put outside on the porticos, verandas, porches, and even in the yard. These unfortunate men shivered in the December cold till someone inside died and created a space for them.

Then, shells started to fall on Lacy House.

"Why are they shelling Lacy House?" Clara asked one of the Union soldiers.

"The Rebs are directing their artillery fire here because they believe the house is occupied by our generals."

"Well, someone needs to tell them it's a hospital. In their haste to harm our Union generals, they're bombing their own injured men, too!"

By the evening of December fifteenth, it was clear the Union would not be triumphant at the Battle of Fredericksburg. The Confederates would claim victory, but looking at the bloodstained battlefield, from that same second-floor balcony of Lacy House, Clara was not sure who had won. The battlefield was strewn with the dead, and darkness seemed to be enveloping so many bodies in both blue and gray uniforms.

As the Union forces retreated, wounded soldiers continued to arrive at Lacy House, and

Clara continued to care for them. She fed them, dressed their wounds, wrote letters to their families, and did her best to keep them warm. When she ran out of bandages, she wrapped their wounds with corn husks.

On Christmas Day, Dr. Cutter stopped by Lacy House to thank Clara for her work and to say goodbye. General Burnside's troops had finished their retreat across the Rappahannock, and Dr. Cutter was traveling with them to their next campsite.

"You have made my birthday special by making the trip to Lacy House," Clara told him.

"Your birthday? Is Christmas Day your birthday?" Dr. Cutter asked.

"Yes, and I feel very fortunate to still be alive and able to care for all these soldiers."

"You know, I heard the injured men on the battlefield talking. Some thought they had died and gone to heaven, and you were an angel who came to help them. At the time, I thought it was just talk, but you really are an angel."

Smiling, he gave Clara a hug.

"Happy Birthday, Angel, and Merry Christmas!"

CONFIDENT BUT CAREFUL

MIKE TRIAL

The June breeze coming in the office window was rich with the scent of new-mown grass. Ann luxuriated in it. And in the knowledge that she had passed all her exams and check rides. She was a licensed pilot. She had hoped her parents could attend the graduation ceremony tomorrow, but when she'd talked to her father on the phone he'd told her it was hay season and with the war on he couldn't hire any help.

Mrs. McIntosh came in and sat down at her desk, her back straight as a ruler.

"Thanks for coming, Ann. Sorry I was delayed."

Ann nodded. "Is there a problem…with me graduating?"

McIntosh smiled. "No, Ann, your academic scores are excellent and your flying is good." Mrs. McIntosh looked out the window, then lit a Chesterfield and blew smoke into the afternoon breeze. "I envy all you girls, class of 1944, going to be Women's Airforce Service Pilots, flying military planes from factory to airfield." She took a drag on her cigarette, hungry for an experience she would never have. "A WASP needs the right combination of confidence and carefulness, Ann. You have it. Maybe just a bit too careful." McIntosh smiled.

Is now the time to tell her? Ann wondered. *Tell her that I love flying the Piper Cubs we fly here but I don't really want to go on to advanced flight training in Texas.*

"But I didn't call you in here to talk about you, Ann. I want to talk to you about your friend Sally Benson." McIntosh stubbed her cigarette out. "Sally didn't pass her written exams. Her test scores averaged 65 percent and you need 70 percent to pass. But her flying skills are very good so I passed her because the WASPs need every available pilot, and they need them right now."

McIntosh picked up a folded piece of paper and tapped it on the desktop. "And there's another reason. This is a summons from a municipal judge in Decatur, Illinois. Seems Sally is married and left Decatur without remembering to tell her husband she was leaving him. He wants her back."

Ann's jaw dropped.

McIntosh put the paper down and lit another cigarette. "But he's not going to get her back. It's now 4:30 Friday afternoon. I'm not going to act on this until Monday morning. And by Monday morning, you and the rest of your classmates will be at Avenger Airfield Texas. No civilian court order has jurisdiction on a military base. Sally will be safe. For a while."

"I had no idea…" Ann said.

McIntosh held up her hand. "Doesn't really matter. What does matter is Sally's piloting. I told you her flying skills are good and they are, but she is a little too confident. That over-confidence will get her into trouble when she's flying bigger planes. In advanced flight training I want you to help her learn to fly with confidence but also with caution. Will you do that for me? And for Sally?"

"I'll do the best I can," Ann said. "But…"

McIntosh stood and guided Ann to the office door. "Do not tell anyone about this. Certainly not Sally. Not until you are checked in at the airfield in Texas. By the way, you'll be leaving for Texas either late tonight or early tomorrow morning. Don't tell anyone about that either."

Ann hurried upstairs to the dorm room she shared with Sally. They were going to be double dating tonight. Dinner and dancing to celebrate graduation. Ann liked her steady date, Allan, but she knew she didn't want a long-term relationship with him. *I'm not sure I want advanced flight training, but going to Texas for training does give me the perfect excuse for not seeing him any more. I can always quit flight school later....*

"You'd better get changed," Sally bubbled. "The guys will be here to pick us up in fifteen minutes."

LARRY, with Allan in the passenger seat, arrived at the dorm in a shiny new 1944 DeSoto. "My dad gave it to me for graduation," Larry smirked. He drove fast through Columbia to campus and parked in front of Gaebler's restaurant. "Dinner with wine," Allan glowed. "To celebrate graduation: us from the University, you two from flight school."

After dinner, Larry, Sally's date, made his way a little unsteadily to the jukebox.

"Play 'In the Mood,'" Sally called to him. Sally liked fast swing tunes. She was a good dancer, and with her Dinah Shore good looks she always drew admiring glances. Ann was pretty sure Larry liked seeing the other guys envious.

As soon as the music started Allan grabbed Sally and pulled her out onto the dance floor. "If you snooze, you lose," he laughed at Larry.

Larry did not ask Ann to dance, which suited Ann fine. *Guess I'm not pretty enough for him*, she thought. She had never really liked Larry much, despite his good looks and his parents' wealth. He was just a little too full of himself. But Sally seemed to like him, and he and Allan were best friends, so the four of them had been double dating since April.

After watching Sally and Allan dance for a moment, Larry leaned across the table and confided to Ann, "I need your help. I want Sally to marry me, but she's been avoiding giving me a yes or no answer."

Ann's heart sank. *Oh my god! I don't want to get mixed up in this. I'm sure Sally has never had any interest in marrying Larry. And she's already married. And she and I are leaving for Texas this weekend.*

"Will you help me?" Larry asked. "Help me get her to say yes."

"Larry, that's very sweet, but I don't think it's the right time to ask Sally...."

His face scrunched up. "Sweet?"

"Larry, this is a really bad time to ask Sally to marry you. We are all shipping out to Texas soon for advanced flight training. Trying to maintain an engagement long distance is almost impossible. It's just not the right time."

He scowled at the tabletop.

The music ended and Sally and Allan came back to the booth. Larry went to the jukebox and played 'Once in a While.' Ann saw Sally shrug, but Sally didn't resist when Larry pulled her onto the dance floor. They seemed to be talking earnestly, as young lovers do.

"Allan, I'm going to the restroom...." Ann said and bolted for the safety of the restroom.

She looked at herself in the mirror. *This is not what I want.* She stood there a long time looking at her reflection.

Suddenly the ladies room door banged open and Sally rushed in shouting, "...get away from me!" She burst into tears and put her face in her hands. "That idiot Larry," she gasped. "I've told him I don't want to get married but he just keeps on and on..."

Ann soothed her the best she could. After a while Ann opened the restroom door a bit. No sign of the boys. She pulled Sally along behind her to the cash register.

"Those two young men left in a huff," Hank Powell, the restaurant owner, told Ann. "Gave me a five dollar bill for a nine dollar tab and stormed out."

"You girls alright?" his wife asked. She was a foot shorter than Hank, and very round. "We're okay," Ann told her. "We'll pay you what we owe. We had an argument."

"I can see that," Mrs. P. said, not unkindly. "How you going to get home?"

Ann drew a deep breath. "Well maybe there's a taxi. We live out at the airport in the Stephens Flight school dorm." She knew she only had three dollars and a quarter in her purse. And she knew Sally never had any money. "Or maybe there's a bus?" she finished uncertainly. She laid all her money on the counter. "I can pay you the rest later." Mrs. Powell swept the money into the cash register. "This will be fine. Consider yourselves paid up."

"It's all my fault," Sally said to no one in particular. "I should never have dated Larry more than twice. Guys always seem think I want to get serious, but I'm just having a good time."

Mrs. P. took Sally's arm, "Calm down, young lady." She turned to Ann, "There's no bus that goes out that way at this hour. I'll drive you to your dorm."

"Gas is rationed, Mabel," Hank told her.

"We've got plenty. It won't take but a gallon to drive these two their dorm."

MRS. POWELL DROVE her 1934 Ford at a steady twenty miles per hour through the empty streets, both hands on the wheel, a look of grim determination on her face. Ann almost laughed out loud. Sally sat in the back seat, silent.

"I can't thank you enough, Mrs. Powell, for driving us home," Ann said.

When they pulled up in the dorm driveway, there was a Columbia city bus parked there with its lights on. Most of the seats seemed to be full. Ann recognized girls from her graduating class.

Mrs. McIntosh bustled up. "You girls get upstairs and get packed right now, one suitcase each, leave the rest of your things on your bed. You're all shipping out tonight for Avenger Field Texas."

"Right now?" Sally said.

McIntosh took her arm and steered her toward the door. "Yes. Right now. Train leaves at midnight."

Sally hurried inside. Mrs. Powell turned to go, but Ann caught her elbow. "Thank you, Mrs. Powell," Ann told her. "You have been very kind."

Just then Larry's DeSoto swerved into the driveway, Allan at the wheel. Larry climbed out of the passenger side, clearly drunk. "Where's Sally? Got to talk to her."

Ann blocked his way, "Go home, Larry. And sober up."

"Get outta the way. You're no help." As he staggered forward, intending to push her aside, Ann dodged him, stepped around him, and gave him a sharp elbow in his side. Off balance, he stumbled, then went down on his rear end. Allan hauled a dazed Larry to his feet. Mrs. P. and Ann confronted them and the boys hesitated. Mrs. McIntosh raced up and the expression on the boys' faces told Ann they realized they didn't have a chance against three determined women. The boys retreated to the car and drove away.

There was applause from the girls on the bus.

"What's going on here?" McIntosh demanded.

"A couple of friends of ours..." Ann said and almost laughed at how that sounded.

"Friends? They didn't act very friendly," McIntosh said.

Mrs. Powell interjected. "Just college boys. They drank too much. Often happens this time of year, celebrating graduation, or drowning their sorrows over getting drafted, or both. They'll forget..."

"You're darned right they will," McIntosh snapped. "Though it really doesn't matter much since these girls are shipping out tonight. You are...?"

"Mabel Powell," the stocky lady said, offering her hand. "My husband and I run Gaebler's restaurant. Speaking of which, I need to get back and help Hank clean up."

Ann waved as Mrs. Powell drove off into the night, still in second gear.

McIntosh pulled Ann into the dorm. "Go get packed—now."

In a few moments Ann and Sally were back downstairs with their suitcases. Mrs. McIntosh walked them out to the bus, then took Ann aside. "Help Sally find that balance between confidence and caution. Just now you showed me you have it. See if you can help Sally find it."

THE NIGHT BREEZE coming in the window of the bus was soft.

Sally said, "Thanks, Ann. I owe you."

"Don't worry about it." Ann said, then let silence settle between them for a time. "But you need to change, become a little more careful."

"I'm not sure I can…"

"Yes you can, we both can." Ann patted her hand. "You be more careful and I'll be more confident."

A TREE WITH NEW LEAVES

LORI YOUNKER

There is a woman now. She comes close to my chair. Her brown eyes see mine. Bending, she lifts my hand, which hangs limp at my side, and gently places it in my lap. I feel the weight of my arm. I am a tree and my arm is a branch of dead wood. I cannot own my hand, nor can I will it to move against gravity.

Good morning. Remember me? The woman sits down on the bed next to my chair. I study her face. She says something to me, but I don't recognize the words. Then, she lifts the good hand and lathers lotion between my fingers, up and over my wrist to my forearms. While she works, she says, *It's me, Yolanda.*

The smell of roses fills the air. My grandmother hated roses, for they meant funeral flowers. Her daddy's suicide. But I love the roses, especially my Lincoln rose, such a tall stem and blooms that open as wide as your face.

I breathe in and out, and the sound of my breathing sounds good in my ears. I feel my chest puff out. I could smile. I mean, the sound of my breathing makes me want to smile, but my face, my cheeks, they won't cooperate.

Señora, I hear the woman's voice again. *The nurse called me. She says you are not eating, Love. This should not be. We are worried about you.* With that, she rubs the heavy hand. She turns my wedding ring round so the setting shows. *Such a pretty ring.*

While I cannot speak, I want to. I would tell her about my ring. Those five little diamonds set in gold on a simple band have been part of my hand since my wedding day. While this woman massages my hands and forearms, I remember my husband, Bill. How wonderful he would ease the tension in my muscles nearly every day. It started with my feet when I was pregnant in those early years and then every morning of forever, he massaged my neck, stiff from sleep.

I feel myself breathing calmly as if he were with me now. My Bill. I wonder why we didn't give each other nicknames. Why didn't we call each other sweetheart and dear? There was always his real name, for his name was the whole of him. Faithful, strong.

The woman is back. She gives me her whole face and smiles at me, as if she were my mother looking down at me in my crib. No, I cannot remember my crib, but I remember my mother. She smiled. Mother always smiled.

Come now, we go to eat. It is the last day before the new year. The woman's voice seems to come from a distance. "*Can you smell the sausage?*

I nod my head. I realize that this is Yolanda. She is speaking Spanish. I recognize many of her words. I open my eyes wide as she puts on my glasses. They pinch behind the ears, but I cannot tell her. I cannot tell her that I will not eat. Trees do not eat. I am a large tree. I lean back in my chair with my face to the sky. I am a tree in the sunshine. Trees do not eat.

There you are, Senora. You see me now. You remember me. You're smiling. She touches my nose with a tap of her index finger, and almost like magic, I know it is time to stand up and to let her guide me to the dining room.

We are the best of friends. Aren't we, Love? You helped me so many years ago, and now I help you. Perhaps you are remembering me, my noisy boys. Angel is in the Air Force and ten years completed already. Tony is an engineer. Tony still talks about you and all you did for him when we came from Guatemala. Why, we only have to say your name, and he must say again that you are his favorite teacher.

I hear the boys' voices in my head, "Teacher!"

I hear my own voice telling my students to always do their best. To have dreams, to have goals, Even small goals will feed the big ones. I am not a tree. I am a teacher.

The woman turns me out the door and down the hall. Ah, at eye level, I read her nametag. Yes, that's what they call it. Nametag. Her name. Yolanda. I can almost feel her name in my mouth. She is important to me.

There are decorations. See the balloons. They are the colors you enjoy. Blue ones. Yellow ones. Her voice is behind me. *Tomorrow it will be two thousand forty-two. Think of that! You have seen a lot in your lifetime. You saw your daughters marry. Remember, no? And you watch all those beautiful grandchildren grow up. Ten of them, remember? How wonderful to be a mother, no?*

I am not a tree. I am a mother.

She guides me to a table. Around us, there are balloons, just as she described. There is music. Yes, I have ten grandchildren. My daughters married good men. My husband loved me. My mother smiled.

My face is wet with my tears. My right hand lifts to my face.

Now don't cry. Yolanda wipes my tears, and I look into her big brown eyes. *Come, eat,* she repeats. *I will sit by you. There is no need to hurry.*

Yolanda lifts a bite of breakfast sausage to my lips. She smiles like my mother. So I will eat.

JOEY

2009

BONNIE ZELENAK

Joey, the new boy from the Philly crowd, is coming up to see me this weekend. He's staying at my house overnight since he has to take the train to get here. And that's a big deal. He's one of the best-looking guys I've ever met. He's smart and works full time, and I can't believe he chose me as his girlfriend.

Mother and Daddy know I'm crazy about him. Everybody knows. I've talked about him endlessly since we met a month ago and he's making the trip just to see me. That my parents would let a stranger stay in our house for the weekend surprises my friends, but it shouldn't. My parents are laid back, and he's a nice guy. A nurse. There's no way we'd be able to do anything, anyway. The bedroom where he'll stay has no door and the whole house squeaks and my parents trust me. That's the rub. It curtails a lot of things I'd like to do.

Knock, knock.

My heart races, and I fly to the door. It's him. He didn't let me down. Our house is several blocks from the train station and now he's here, standing on the porch holding a duffle bag. Smiling at me, his deep blue eyes take me in.

"Hi," I say, suddenly shy.

"Hi, Lily. It's nice to see you."

"Thanks. Come in."

Mother greets him with a cheerful voice. "You must be Joey. Lily's been looking forward to seeing you. Can I get you an iced tea?"

"That'd be nice. Thanks, Mrs. Green."

He gives me a quick hug when she goes to the kitchen and I lean in to kiss him. He turns his head and I manage a glancing kiss on his cheek. What's that about? When I pull back, he must have noticed my frown, but he only raises his brows.

After depositing his overnight bag in the upstairs bedroom, we head out to my jalopy, a yellow Chevy Neon that's been around the block too many times. "Want to see Stacy and the gang?" I ask, knowing he likes my friends, my shore buddies. He's a newcomer to the Philly crowd we hang out with at Beach Haven, and he's an exceptional addition. Tall, with dark brown wavy hair, sapphire blue eyes, and employed. He's a nurse and not shy about saying so. And he's smart, not a wise guy like the others.

"Yeah. I'd like that," he says.

We lower our windows and head out. It's a beautiful summer day, the air is cool, and the sky is so clear it almost hurts your eyes. "They'll be at the bowling alley this afternoon. Let's surprise them," I say.

"Nice. Who else will be there? I mean, of your friends I've already met?"

"Jean and Kerry, probably. Some other kids from school will be there, but they're not my close friends. There's always a crowd."

We pull into the lot and work our way to the back lanes where my friends hang out. Stacy looks up, clears her throat, and says, "Joey," keeping a straight face.

"Stacy," he nods, mimicking her serious expression and tone. They're playing off each other, and without saying so, it's about him spending the weekend at my house. She's trying to be funny, but it's weird.

We're halfway through the first game when Donna strolls over to say hello. She never stops by our lanes, but someone new and handsome caught her attention. She's smart, her family's loaded, and she'll attend an Ivy League. Her clothes are Hollister or Abercombie and Fitch, she pays big bucks for her attire, and she swishes while showing it off. She's tall and slender with long blonde hair—and a big nose. I'm tall and slender with long blonde hair, too, but my clothes don't look like hers, and my car neither looks nor runs like her little '08 Triumph convertible. My dad doesn't make as much money as hers, and although she always says hello, we're not friends. What's she doing at our alley?

Joey's eyes are glued to her, and she's getting off on it. She knows he came with me, but she's strutting around like he's hers, and he's loving it.

I'm the girl boys are interested in. I'm used to it, and I like it, but I don't flaunt it. But it's not happening today. Today, I'm the girl watching my guy step aside. He likes Donna and her expensive clothes and her skinny body. He's panting over her Versace blouse, her personal bowling shoes, and the Fendi Teen combat boots she tossed down beside my Keds.

Forget him. I'm yanking off my bowling shoes and getting out of here. I can't hang around and watch some skank steal my guy.

But he's not really mine. He's a guy who's a friend of my friends, a guy I recently met, a guy I don't really know. And I don't really like.

Joey watches Donna as I pack up. She glances my way, wearing an exuberant smile.

"Want him?" I ask, voice harsh, conveying annoyance.

"I'll take a crack at him if you're done with him," Donna says smoothly, glancing in Joey's direction.

"You can have him. I'll deliver his stuff to your house in an hour. Take him home and tell him never to call me again. You'll be doing me a favor."

"Gladly," she purrs, walking over and sitting on his lap.

I stomp out of the place, drive home, shove his crap into his duffle and drop it off at her house. All within thirty minutes. Joey calls as I'm driving to Donna's, but I block his number, never wanting to hear from him again.

On Sunday, my phone rings and I don't recognize the number, so I pick up. Joey's on the line and says, "Hold on, Lily. Don't hang up. Please." He's using Donna's phone, the lunk.

"What do you want?"

"How am I going to get back to the train station?" he asks, sounding desperate.

"Like I care? Have Donna take you, dummy."

"She won't. Says she's late for work. Her dad left the house and her mom doesn't drive."

"Not my problem. Don't call me again," I say, but hear him pleading, so I hesitate.

"Come on, Lily, I need to get back to my job. I can't lose my job. I take care of my mom. Come on, it's important."

"You can walk. The train station's not that far, less than two miles. Have Donna draw you a map," I say, and hang up.

Twelve Years Later

I thought about Joey off and on that summer, but he soon faded from importance. He was a handsome, if insensitive character, and handsome alone never cut it for me. Every guy I've fallen for since has been a decent man, a man with a soul and a heart and a brain. Intelligence always wins out when I analyze what I find appealing. Regardless of their assets, however, I've grown tired of every relationship I've had, not that there were that many. And we say goodbye as friends.

This week I'm attending the 2021 World Heart and Cardiothoracic Surgery Conference in Bangkok and have settled into my seat in the auditorium, waiting for the plenary session to begin. The Avani Atrium Bangkok Hotel is stunning—and cheap. I can't believe the deal I got, and the luxury in which I'll be living for the next five nights.

The speaker walks onto the stage and arranges his microphone. Several colleagues set up the video equipment, and there's twenty minutes to spare. He's obviously well prepared and his colleagues cater to his wishes. He must be up there in the stratosphere of respected surgeons, the way they scurry around, assuring that the arrangements are as he wishes. He laughs with them and sends them on their way, then focuses on his notes.

Rebecca nudges me and whispers, "He's a looker, Lil. See if you can catch his eye. Maybe he's available."

I shake my head and smirk. Becca is always pushing me at somebody. She's happily married and thinks everybody else should be, too. Truth be told, life as a female cardiac surgeon has diminished my playfulness. What I want at the end of most days is a quiet evening at home. By myself.

The speaker lifts his head and looks directly at me. Holy smokes, I'm in his line of sight, but he's staring at me and—woah—the intensity behind those blue eyes sends a jolt of heat right to my core. He lifts his brows and sucks half of his bottom lip into his mouth. Holding my gaze, he leans across the podium and pulls his index finger toward himself, a gesture that could only mean, *come here.*

I look at Becca, and she's wearing an outrageous smile. "Go. He's calling you. Go!"

"What the hell?" I whisper, trying not to move my lips, keeping my eye on him and planting myself in my seat.

"At least see what he wants," she says.

He smiles and mouths the words, "Come here. Please," and he again motions for me to join him.

"This is crazy," I mumble, standing and straightening my skirt. I slide out of the aisle and head to the stage as he walks to the stairs leading down. Okay, I'll walk over to those stairs. And I'll find out what he wants.

I arrive at the steps. He walks down, touches my elbow, and chuckles. "Aren't you Lily... um, hold on? Lily Green, from Trenton?"

"That's my name, and that's where I grew up. I'm sorry, have we met?"

"Years ago. You told me to find my own way back to the train station. You basically told me to take a walk."

"Sorry? I'm not sure you've got the right person."

"Oh, you're the right person. If you're Lily Green, you're the right person. What are you doing here?"

"Attending the conference." Duh.

"You're a surgeon?" he asks, the thought apparently bewildering him.

"That's why I'm here," I say, turning, ready to head back to my seat.

"Who paid your way through Med School?" he asks, the question so personal it glues me to the spot.

"My parents, grants, and lots of loans," I say, growing annoyed at his forwardness. "Why? Who paid yours?"

"Donna's dad. Remember Donna?" He asks, eyes sparkling. It seems he's holding his breath, waiting for me to recognize something.

And then it hits me. "Joey? Oh, my God. You're Joey?"

"Go by Joseph now, but Joe works, too."

"Donna's father put you through med school?" I ask with a smirk. "Lucky you."

"He sure did."

"Is Donna here?"

"Nah, haven't seen her in years. Hardly saw her while I was in Med School. She got fed up and left."

"Was that your plan all along?" I ask, laughing, unable to be pissed at his audacity so many years after he blew me off.

"Would you hate me if I said 'yes'?"

"I might think you're a conniving son of a gun, but I wouldn't hate you."

"Good," he says. "I called you, you know. Lots of times."

"Pfft. I wouldn't know. I blocked your calls. For forever."

"I know," he replies, smiling. "Can I make it up to you? Buy you a drink after the session?"

I look at Becca, who's wearing a huge smile. She'd want me to say yes. "Sure. Why not? Oh, wait, is there a *Mrs. Joseph*? And are there kids?" I'm not interested in connecting with a conniver a second time around.

"No. I never remarried. Never had kids. Been busy, you know?"

"Yeah, I know. It's hard to find time to visit with friends, to just relax."

"Let's catch up, Lily. Visit with an old friend and relax," he suggests, voice dipping to a gruff tenor.

"I'd like that." Joey has grown up, and I'd love to play catch-up.

NONFICTION

Photo Credit: Gail Denham

NONFICTION JUDGE

Donna Duly Volkenannt

Donna Duly Volkenannt is a wife, mother, grandmother, and breast cancer survivor. She writes essays, poems, nonfiction, short stories, and re-enactment scripts for cemetery walks. Her work has appeared in local, national, and international publications. Volkenannt has received numerous awards including the Erma Bombeck Global Humor Award and the Pikes Peak National League of American Pen Women's flash fiction award, and she was a top-ten finalist in the Steinbeck short story competition. A native Saint Louisan, Donna lives in Saint Peters but spends time in her country cabin in Osage County. She's currently at work on her first novel.

SECRETS FROM THE PORTER PANTRY

FOOD 'N' SUCH

MILLICENT HENRY PORTER

According to my calculations, in the last 71 years I've eaten approximately 78,000 meals. Although I'm sure that doesn't even begin to accommodate the number of extra snacks I've devoured.

My food choices for the first seventeen years were, by necessity, influenced by the family I grew up in, where we lived and how tight the budget was that month. Momma was a frugal cook who interned during the Depression. Heaven help you if you hated leftovers. But she baked heart-stopping lemon meringue pie, kept the cookie jar filled with oatmeal cookies, and made our sandwiches with homemade potato bread.

My husband still requests one of her old standbys, a meal we called "Mrs. Garber's skillet dinner." Momma melted shortening in a huge skillet, browned pork steak and topped the meat with potatoes, onions, carrots and cabbage. And for holidays I always make her "Apple Poof" dessert. She melted marshmallows in pineapple and orange juice, mixed in whipped cream and shredded apples, and arranged the pudding-like mixture between layers of vanilla wafers.

Daddy contributed to our diet in other interesting ways. He loved to hunt and expected Momma to cook whatever he bagged. We learned to eat squirrel, rabbit, frog legs, quail, duck, and assorted species of fish. His taste buds were exotic for a Nebraska boy; he introduced me to pickled herring, tidbits of raw steak seasoned with salt and pepper, and beef tongue sandwiches spread with horseradish which reminds me . . .

Every spring Daddy planted two enormous gardens and delighted in trying a new vegetable each growing season. The year he planted horseradish as the experimental crop remains as vivid today as it was sixty years ago. Harvest time had arrived. Daddy pulled the long green and leafy tops of the horseradish plants out of the ground to reveal fat bulbous carrot-like roots, lots of them. He cut off the leaves and scrubbed the roots until they gleamed like white icicles on a wintry day. In the kitchen, he attached Momma's metal food grinder to one end of the gate leg table and inserted the sprocket for a fine grind. A shallow bowl waited beneath the grinder.

"Please, pretty please, can I turn the handle?" I begged.

Momma and Daddy exchanged a look.

Daddy patted my sausage curls and gave me a gentle push. "Hook-ie," he said. "This is dirty work, no fun at all. You go on out and play. Just don't disremember to come home when the six o'clock whistle blows."

I pouted, then reluctantly pedaled over to Steven's house where we spent a couple of hours climbing trees and rigging up a pulley system that enabled us to send snacks and silly handwritten notes to each other from our perches in the Sugar Maple tree. When the quitting time siren blew, I abandoned Steven and raced down Third Street to our house.

At the front door, I heard great gusts of laughter coming from the kitchen. I hurried inside, eager to find out what was so funny.

Daddy called out to me. "Oh brave child, enter if you dare." His voice was wheezy, almost like he was crying. Then he choked up and he and Momma started to giggle all over again.

Halfway across the living room I asked, "What's so doggone . . . " Before I could say the word funny, it hit me. The very air in the house was fiery hot. Each inhalation made the tender lining of my nose burn. And my eyes wept to protect themselves from the hazardous fumes. But I was determined to make it to the kitchen. I pulled my T-shirt over my head and felt along the sectional couch, past the dining room table to the archway of the kitchen.

Once there, I risked a peek. What a sight. Numerous bowls, filled to overflowing with ground horseradish, littered the kitchen counter. Momma turned the handle of the grinder. She stood as far away from it as possible with her apron pressed against her nose and mouth. Over the top of a ruffle, I could see her soft brown eyes, red rimmed and watery.

Daddy had stripped down to his wife beater and rolled his ancient khakis up above the knees. The hand he used to poke the roots into the mouth of the grinder was enveloped in a plastic yellow glove. On his nose, he wore my nose plugs heretofore used only for swimming; a pair of safety glasses from his Chemistry class covered his eyes. Their skin appeared bright red and blotchy. Still they laughed. I could stand no more and bolted to the backyard. That's where my sister, Priscilla found me when she came home from her babysitting job. When she asked what was wrong, I simply pointed to the house.

For supper, Daddy grilled hamburgers outside on the old rock fireplace, and Momma made ice cream floats with Orange Crush. When the stars came out, we roasted marshmallows over the dying embers. By midnight we had given up all hope of sleeping in the house. The fumes were even more toxic and took your breath away. So Daddy set up the musty canvas tent while Momma dashed into the house for blankets and pillows. I slept surrounded by the flicker of lightning bugs and the croak of locusts, in the warm, safe arms of my family. Since that long ago day, I have never once been tempted to plant horseradish in my garden.

CANCER IN A COVID WORLD

LISA PULLEN KENT

They called her Barbie, an apt moniker for her given name. A real-live Barbie doll, she was tall, voluptuous, blonde. But she also carried herself with the elegance of a Barbara. Movie-star glamour. Dressed to the nines and turning heads. She made you feel important when she bestowed her attention on you; she was all yours. Her eyes held an almost mischievous spark, while her gorgeous, wide-mouthed smile lifted only one side. Her laugh was sensuous, subtle.

Dad emailed on Monday.

"Good morning, kids. Our dear Barbie passed through the veil last night about 9:15 pm Seattle time. She never woke up again since she went to sleep Thursday evening. It was a very blessed and peaceful passing. No more pain and trauma to her little body."

There are five of them, my dad and his siblings, stair-stepping, like a single slinky, one child pouring into the next: girl-boy-boy-girl-girl. Trisha, Bill, Maynard—my father, then Barbara, and Pammy, the youngest. Maybe it was their humble beginnings, growing up with working class parents in a small mountain town, poor, but happy. Maybe it was my grandparents' tough love or the necessity of relying on family, but whatever the reason, my father and his sibs are tight. Throughout life's adversities, into their 70s and 80s now, they've remained best friends and one another's fiercest champions. They have faced everything together. They conquered everything together.

Until pancreatic cancer.

The last time I saw her was six months ago when I flew up for Grandma's funeral, six months and a lifetime ago–before the coronavirus pandemic. The matriarch of our clan lived until she was nearly 104, so long that immortality seemed a real possibility.

I hadn't visited Aunt Barbara since her diagnosis, but I'd seen photos. I'm familiar with how this disease ravages the body and steals hopes for survival. But, reassurances from my family emphasized Barbara's resilience. Her spirits were fully intact, her faith strong, her smile as radiant as ever.

And so it seemed as she made her appearance, chic in a pale silk pantsuit and leather ankle boots topped with a floor-length fur draped over her shoulders to ward off the chill. Still strikingly beautiful, cancer had chiseled her porcelain features into a sharp likeness, a sculpture of herself, without any rounded curves. The gauntness in her face pained me, and when I wrapped my arms around her fragile bird bones, the ephemeral nature of her body resonated within mine. The tears I would not show her collected under my closed lids.

I pictured Barbara, circa 1970-something in a photo snapped on the beach in Southern California. She's posed seductively next to a white Jaguar. The blue sky merges with the blue ocean and her golden Breck-girl hair whips in the wind. All savvy sophistication, she embodied the beauty I aspired to in my little girl hero-worship.

Gathering to remember Grandma, we spent our days circled up on sectionals, recliners, and pulled-up kitchen chairs. Hours of conversation, catching up on years-worth of life, reminiscing about the past. Barbara stayed, though sometimes, succumbing to exhaustion, she'd curl up on a stretch of couch, unwilling to miss anything. Her husband, Richard unfolded a soft blanket and tucked it around her edges, patting her gently while continuing the conversation. Even if she drifted in and out, she was still there. She was still there, dammit.

I noticed with amusement through the waning of the hours that she wasn't the only one who dozed. At some point or other, each of my elders nodded off. With arms crossed, chin dropping to chest or sitting erect and perfectly still, eyes closed, they drifted. If supported, a head might loll back, a mouth open slightly, a soft snore emerge. Upon waking, the process of re-orienting played across their faces and I was tickled to notice they hadn't even known they'd slept.

The catnaps obviously granted these septa and octogenarians a second wind, for their stamina far outpaced mine. I retreated to the quiet darkness of Aunt Trisha's bedroom, wiped out by 10:00 pm on my last night. Intending only to rest my eyes, I crashed hard despite the cascading laughter coming through the walls. Blearily, I roused when light flooded the room through a crack in the door.

I jumped up, seeing it was Barbara.

"You're not leaving, are you?"

"No," she whispered. "Just getting my coat. Go back to sleep."

"But, but," I struggled to keep my eyes open and get the words out. "Don't go without saying goodbye," I said. "Promise!? I'll get up. I want to see you before you go."

She eased the door shut with a soft click and I laid my head back down, fighting to stay alert. Even as sleep tried to pull me under, I kept my focus half-cocked toward the door, intuiting how like her it would be to slip out quietly so as not to wake me.

Later, I emerged to find everyone still chatting leisurely around the dining table. Except for Barbara. Richard had taken her home.

Time was up. Tomorrow morning I'd leave for the airport and I knew in my gut I would not be back to say goodbye. Considering it had taken me years to make it up to Seattle from my Midwestern home, the crushing knowledge landed: I would not see her again in this lifetime.

Not in person, at least. She did appear in a small window on my computer screen. The lockdown of March 2020 birthed a weekly family Zoom, a calamitous Brady Bunch-style cacophony of technical gymnastics that proved to be quite entertaining. Close-ups of foreheads, noses, and blank walls, interference and background noise, competing conversations both on and off the digital airwaves kept me in stitches.

"Can you hear me?"

"We can't hear you."

"You have to click unmute!"

"Can you see me?"

"I can't see anybody."

"Who said that?"

A scan of the familiar, beloved faces revealed our shared genetics. Dad and Uncle Bill, ruggedly handsome, channeled my sweet Grandpa, Shorty he was called, gone now some 22 years. I compared my sisters' faces with my cousins,' finding the same eyes, cheekbones, smiles. Across the generations, across the country, we gathered in this virtual space, in real time, in a way we never could in a physical sense. We compared notes about work, school, COVID developments from state to state, how we were all coping. We scheduled around Barbara's chemotherapy treatments, and she attended as much as she could, bantering along with the rest of us.

Between one Zoom and the next, horrible, unrelenting pain took her to the hospital. Just like that, she was admitted. The tumors over-taking her digestive system had obstructed nutrients and now were beginning to prohibit organ function. She'd been here before, deathly ill, touch and go, but she had always rebounded. But this time was different. This time there would be no rallying.

Even knowing the eventuality, it is never palatable. It is never acceptable.

But here it was.

Visits were allowed, but only Richard and Pammy. Palliative care and end of life decisions had to be made and as excruciatingly difficult as that was, navigating it all through a global pandemic held heart-breaking ramifications. The other sibs were too high risk themselves to visit, and in my father's case, too far away. Travel restrictions and time limits applied. I thought of stories I'd heard of nurses who, acting as proxy, held the hands of dying patients when their loved ones couldn't be with them. The stark image I'd seen of an elderly husband outside the window of his wife's hospital room, desperate to comfort her through the glass, is burned into my memory. I'd read about FaceTime death vigils, FaceTime confessions, FaceTime farewells.

For Barbie and Richard and everyone who loved her, the most significant blessing came when she was discharged and got to come home. She would not be isolated in a sterile hospital. She would not be alone at the end of her life. Once settled, on one last morning of lucidity, she was showered with texts and emails and videos and songs from her large family. She talked with her siblings and gave them the goodbyes they desperately needed.

On the small screen of a phone held close to her face, my dad told his little sister how much he loved her, then asked tenderly, "Barbie, are you afraid?"

"Oh, nooooo," she cooed peacefully. "I'm not scared at all."

It was permission. Her permission to them. If she could walk into the next world without fear, her family could let her go.

I've learned the most brilliant epiphany of approaching death is the invitation to embrace life fully. The mundane becomes holy, the simple act of breathing, a gift, to love and be loved, a sacrament.

And so, she died on a Sunday night, and on Monday afternoon, our next Zoom began with the usual fits and starts as folks logged on, checked their mics, and adjusted camera angles. Simultaneous greetings and conversations zig-zagged across the gallery. The geometric family tree took shape as new people blinked into existence in their individual cubicles. There were jokes about how Richard's love of Jack-in-the-Box tacos required a detour on the way home from the hospital, followed by the question, "Jack-in-the-Box has tacos?" which was followed by incredulous laughter.

Then we got down to the hard stuff.

"What can we do for you?" everyone asked Richard.

"I can't believe it," he said.

"It doesn't seem real," Pammy sobbed, despondent at the loss of her sister and best friend.

With minimal detail, they told us the story, how once home from the hospital, they'd never left Barbara's side. When she took her last breath, they were there. She passed three days nearly to the minute after slipping into unconsciousness.

"I'm so proud of her," Richard said and rubbed the stubble of his unshaven chin.

His understated grief not only triggered my own, but the empathy I felt for him brought me to the ugly cry. I covered my mouth with my hand and let the tears come. Lately, my emotions are scrubbed up raw. Tender, like new skin. My nerve endings fire all the time. I feel everything without a buffer, as if there are no more desensitizing layers laid down with busy, distracted, numbing activity.

The pandemic has stripped me clean.

This, too, might be a gift, though it hardly seems so when it hurts this badly. Everything shines with meaning now. Grief begs me to take it in and absorb the simple, extraordinary presence of love, wherever and however it shows up.

The funeral will be live-streamed via teleconferencing software, much like our family Zooms. Music, prayers, memories will be shared. A eulogy. A slideshow. Through the window of our computer screens we'll view the service from our living rooms. We'll reach out for comfort through the interwebs. We'll mourn together while we're apart which seems nearly poetic in its brutality. We cannot be together, even to commemorate our loved one's life, yet nothing can keep us apart. The connection is stronger and resonates beyond any tangible barrier.

Family ties cannot be severed by cancer or COVID or even death.

PICKLES? MAYBE. PARSLEY? MAYBE NOT.

FRANK MONTAGNINO

The phone rang at 1:30, just as I was finishing lunch. The ID on the screen read E.J. Johnson, so I knew it was my sister Roberta, whose name is not Johnson. She has told me several times why she keeps her home phone listed under Johnson, but I can never remember. Anyway, I gave her the standard greeting. "Hello, Johnson."

Her reply was, "Have you had your tea yet?"

She was referring to the envelope of tea bags she had mailed to me a few days earlier. The tea bags contained something called Parsley Tea, which I had never heard of, but which she touted as being a curative for aches and pains including those caused by arthritis, rheumatism, and just plain overdoing old, underused muscles. I'd recently been doing a lot of overdoing as I'd explained to her in one of our weekly telephone talks.

With spring recently sprung, my wife handed me a list of long-procrastinated chores like mulching yard areas that had never before seemed to need mulch. That of course, entailed the lifting and lugging of many 40-pound bags, not to mention putting down the rubber edging and the plastic weed shield prior to spreading the mulch. Anyway, I was discussing the anticipated muscle soreness with my sister when she interrupted.

"You should get some parsley tea. My neighbor across the road, Ann, told me about it and it really works."

"Is this like pickle juice," I asked. Years ago, she had recommended drinking a slug of pickle juice to alleviate leg cramps. I'd pooh-poohed that suggestion until one occasion when a monumental leg cramp in the middle of the night just wouldn't go away. Out of desperation I grabbed a bottle of pickles from the fridge and gulped down a healthy swig of the juice. To my surprise and relief, minutes later the cramp was gone. Remarkable! Aspirin might have accomplished the same result, but not for at least an hour. Next time she phoned I acknowledged the success of her home remedy. To her credit she didn't gloat too much except to mention "the cherries."

Years before she had advised me to eat cherries to cure occasional sieges of gout. I never tried that remedy because I was already taking anti-gout pills prescribed by an endocrinologist with an actual license to practice medicine. On the other hand, I admit to modifying my sister's remedy into a precautionary treatment. I now ward off gout by including at least two maraschino cherries in every homemade Manhattan.

Don't get me wrong. My sister is a wonderful person, one of the two best sisters in the world. But to be honest, she has this odd quirk when it comes to food and cooking. It first became evident back when we were just kids. We're of Italian descent, so it was traditional that every Sunday dinner featured pasta of some sort. Somewhere along the line, Roberta started putting chili flakes on her macaroni – an abomination exceeded only by barbarians who put pineapple on pizza. We tried to cajole her out of it.

"You realize we're Italian, not Mexican."

She ignored our comments and continued to ruin countless pasta dishes.

Later, perhaps caused by seeing too many Bill Cosby commercials, she became enamored of Jell-O. We didn't notice that aberration while we were living with our parents and Roberta didn't do the cooking. But after she married it became evident that Jell-O was a featured part of every meal she hosted. I have no proof of this, but I always suspected Jell-O was the main course when she and her hubby were dining alone.

Because we live many miles apart, I didn't suffer from her Jell-O fetish except on rare family get-togethers where a plate of the jiggly stuff was always in evidence on her table – often camouflaged with marshmallows or Dream Whip or infused with bits of fruit. I once sent her a Jell-O mold that I found in a novelty shop. It produced a quivering blob of Jell-O in the shape of a human brain. Luckily, the occasion never happened when I had to eat the end product.

Jell-O wasn't her only food foible. Her New Year's Eve celebrations always featured the consumption of cabbage. That's not unusual, I know, since millions of people share the superstition that eating cabbage on New Year's assures good luck and good fortune during the upcoming year. I'm sure others also emulate her by putting a purse containing a few dollars out on the front stoop and retrieving it after the clock strikes midnight. If the cash is still in the purse, she maintains, you will have money for the upcoming year. The impact in her case is minimized because she lives out in the country in a house set back at least a thousand yards from any roving purse purloiners.

While a lot of people share her cabbage fetish, I'll bet not many emulate her other New Year's Eve ritual of walking out the front door, around the house (in the dark, just before midnight, mind you) and back in the front door. She has explained the rationale behind this weirdness, but I've purged it from my memory.

Roberta's food obsessions aren't limited to New Year's Eve. Once she called to inform me that it was a special day when I had to eat cream puffs. And she always calls on St. Joseph's Day to inquire about our intake of fava beans. I've never asked, but I'd be amazed if she doesn't have one in her purse right now to insure good luck.

It was never clear just when my sister's strange proclivities toward foods veered off into the curative arts. Her metamorphosis into a shaman was gradual; her prescription of Parsley Tea to cure aches and pains being just the latest.

Since she had gone to the trouble and expense of mailing me the tea bags, I felt duty bound to taste a cup. I followed the instructions for creating "a medicinal tea" and let the bag steep for twelve minutes. Parsley Tea, it turns out, doesn't produce a brownish liquid like ordinary tea. Even after steeping it remained a clear, ominous-looking brew that immediately activated my gag reflex. Cautiously, I added a spoonful of sugar and took a small sip. Contrary to my preconceived notion, it wasn't horrible. Bad, but not horrible. I was even able to manage a larger swallow. But that was all. Familial duty fulfilled I was free to dump the rest of the cup into the sink with a conscience as clear as the tea itself. Too bad my muscles weren't sore enough to evaluate its curative properties, but regardless, I'm certain Parsley Tea will not be listed among my favorite drinks or remedies.

It's okay that my shaman sister whiffed on her latest recommendation. Her spot-on advice about the efficacy of pickle juice to chase away cramps has me forever indebted to her. I would just add this disclaimer for any readers who would like to try this remedy. Make sure you use the juice from sweet relish or sweet gherkins. A gulp of dill juice would be worse than the cramps.

THE PLEASURE OF DANGER

ANNE GIFFORD

In my youth, I might have pushed the edge a tad when it came to doing anything that could possibly be dangerous. I was naïve and infallible, so I might not have had a second thought on whether something could be precarious.

Now that I am older, I've become more cautious and aware of taking risks, even with my normal daily activities of living. For example, walking down a flight of stairs and looking straight ahead, instead of looking down at each step. As a nurse, I can see the potential danger where one wrong step can lead to a disastrous outcome. It could send me tumbling down the staircase and result into a cascade of potential consequences, such as: a fracture, surgery, an impending blood clot in the leg or lung, pneumonia, an infected incision, and death. On the other hand, what would I have missed out on if I had not taken a potentially dangerous risk?

I think about the time I went whitewater river rafting in Montana. After gearing up in wetsuits and life preservers, our group received a comprehensive safety lecture that addressed falling out the raft while running the rapids. My chest tightened and a chill ran down my back as fear weakened my knees.

I turned to my friends, Jane and Bob Smith (their real names) and hesitantly asked, "Are we sure we still want to do this?" Bob smiled with excitement as Jane responded, "Of course we do. Now get in the boat." I obediently followed my 85-year-old friends and climbed in the raft.

After a series of mild rapids through shallow sandy based waters, I felt comfortable, confident, and very safe. Pleasure filled my sense of well-being as we floated along the calm waterway.

Suddenly our guide swung his oar around him, shifted his body to one side of the raft, and yelled for everyone to grab their oars and follow his directions. The intensity of his command was daunting. Directly ahead was a drop off between large boulders and roaring white-water rapids. I gasped with fear as we succumbed to a series of fast-flowing mini-falls bordered with fallen tree branches. The roaring sound of the rushing waters appeared eerily frightening. The voluminous sounds prevailed, blocking out any reassuring casual conversation.

I was now facing the ultimate danger of my life and my comfort level was threatened. It was too late for me to back out of this mind-boggling adventure. I envisioned myself flipping out of the raft and drowning in the mountain river rapids. Eventually, my limp body may be found after the fish had nibbled on it. My appendages would become bloody red and pink flaps of tissue amid bony protuberances. Or perhaps my body would wash ashore for the fox and coyotes to finish cleaning the meat off my bones.

I grabbed my oar and leaned in as I tightened my calves and thighs securely against the inside of the raft and firmly planted my feet. Giving my full attention to our guide, my heart pounded against my chest as the raft buoyantly bounced along with the river's intense speed and weight.

The guide continued to yell out instructions as we dug our paddles in the torrents of water, forcing us toward huge boulders. Cooperation and expediency prevailed; this was not the time to ask questions. Waves of water splashed over the sides, drenching us as the river pounded and spun us around in circles. Some riders screamed with excitement while others intensified their concentration in the battle of life or death.

Then . . . what seemed to be forever, the rapids suddenly subsided as we floated along in the gently flowing river. All was calm. I looked around and counted to see if we lost anyone. Smiles and laughter suddenly replaced the anxious screams. Feeling exhilarated with a sense of accomplishment, I turned to my friends, Jane and Bob, "That was so much fun! Let's do it again." Oh, such is the pleasure of danger.

CHRISTMAS TREES PAST

WANITA MARIE HUMPHREY

To farm dwellers, a Christmas tree was a cedar that you chopped down on your own property. Likely, you would have staked one out in late October or November, but what was lush and green then could, or very likely would, be as brown as dead grass come mid-December. This would lead to the necessity to find a new *perfect tree*.

From the time we were old enough, probably eight and twelve, my brother, Jim, and I would take the ax and set off across the *holler* in search of our Christmas tree.

Too short, too tall, too thin, too brown—Jim would lose patience with me—and to be fair, I was awfully picky and he had been pretty good about it all, but after a while, Jim would drop the ax and stomp off toward the house. It was pretty well determined before we set out that this is what would happen—it usually did.

I would eventually find *the tree*, chop it down and drag it back to the house, sometimes as twilight set in.

Mom wouldn't brook any fussin' so there were few words of recrimination between Jim and me at that point. Besides, we were close, *twins,* as he had the temerity to be born on my fourth birthday, even almost the same time of day.

All was well, and the tree was decorated while enjoying the hot chocolate mom always made.

I got married. My husband and I now got our tree, a cedar, which we chopped down—he just persevered on the hunt until I was happy with *our choice*.

Jim would always tease me about that tree when he visited. "Brown as dead leaves. You could read a newspaper through that one. Had to cut too much off the bottom. Isn't part of the top missing?"

I always expected his good-natured jibes and would give back just as good when I looked at his tree.

Time passes so quickly. Jim and I are old. Our children are grown. Our grandchildren are quickly growing up. Neither of us has cut down a cedar tree for many years. We both have beautiful artificial trees, even though we both swore we would never have one of *those things* in our house. Each year, during the holidays, when we are together, the subject of Christmas tree hunting comes up.

"You always wanted to look at every tree on the farm."

"You always wanted to take the first one we saw."

"That thing you drug home would have half the needles wore off."

"At least I brought something home."

And then the laughter would start.

Each year when I decorate my tree, the last ornament I hang is a silver and blue one that has the three wise men on it. It is one that was always placed on those cedar trees so long ago. It always brings tears —happy ones. It reminds me of wonderful years, family love, and precious memories of Christmas trees past.

RETIREMENT REFLECTIONS FROM MY STANDING DESK

LYNN STRAND MCINTOSH

I didn't plan on growing old, at least not this quickly. They say that time goes faster as we age because of our altered perception of time. We either process time in the moment, or as recollections of past time. The future is a time that hasn't yet happened so can only be imagined. I have never been much of a planner, the majority of my life I tended to live in the moment just enjoying the ride. When you're young almost everything is new and is going to happen and when you're older more has happened than will; hence this second guessing of time. I am no Einstein, but to me this kind of relativity makes sense. As an old lady, I can't help but examine my life's surprising twists and turns. I have relatively few regrets but never about the relatives I beget. My primary occupation was as a parent, regardless of whatever careers I dabbled in. The second definition of "occupation" is more relevant here - that is "the action, state, or period of occupying or being occupied by a military force". My occupying force was five boys, camouflaged in cuteness and armed to their smiling teeth. I was the resident Officer in Charge, anchored to my desk in the kitchen, dispensing sustenance and supervision. This was a stand-up desk before they were popular. I spent decades clinging bare-knuckled to the sides of my kitchen sink through the ups and downs of motherhood. Now, with more time on my hands,

I occasionally wonder if I would have signed up for this job if I could have imagined the future. Would I have even fit the qualifications?

WANTED: Someone to love and care for five boys in perpetuity, a person who enjoys growth, extending one's physical boundaries and timely delivery of goods. Their timely delivery, not your's. Salary commensurate with experience, although neither is applicable. A nine month probationary period consists of nausea, weight gain, swollen ankles, and anxiety. Additional duties may consist of heartburn, fatigue, constipation and related hemorrhoids. Probation ends with prolonged expulsion of future staff through a previous small private area. Neither of which will remain small or private. Extensive and interminable hours during this period do not qualify for overtime or any other pay. This probationary period can be reinstated with occasional lapse of memory or wine option.

DUTIES AFTER PROBATIONARY PERIOD: These are too numerous to be listed but included are the daily planning, shopping, preparing and serving of foodstuffs required by your underlings. The staff will most likely not appreciate said choices but will regardless finish at a record pace and move on to mess up another work area while you clean up your main office for the fifth time that day. Hazards may include more weight gain due clean up duties, as you may not have eaten and may finish everything on their plates while standing at your desk with running water. While these tasks will remain your first priority and will take up the bulk of your day, your number two duties can occur at any inconvenient time. Diapering and wiping manuals are not necessary as skills are taught by expediency. Delay of these duties can extend to more of the same on appendages, floors or walls. Best method tested seems to be staff grabbing your legs while you bend over your satellite desk (also with running water) and wave good by to the outcomes. Purchasing, preparing and flushing of foodstuffs will consume approximately 30% of your day, well, your waking day.

Please see extensive notes for exceptions on times and fecal frequencies.

CONTINUED EMPLOYMENT OPTIONS: There are no options, however all duties continue. As your position progresses there will be no promotions or increase in pay. Junior staff will be critical of all attempts at anything and will learn new measures to try your skills and patience. Patience, a strong gag reflex and a sense of humor are beneficial to applicants and staff. You may be required to attend instructional meetings with teachers, clergy, perfect parents of perfect kids (PPPK) and an occasional police officer. Perfect parents of perfect kids (PPPK) are those whose children would not be in trouble if it were not for your children. These critical consultants will evaluate your commitment to helping them get through these trying times. You may be required to nod in agreement while biting your tongue and writing a check to the appropriate tutor, lawyer or hotel chain. The possibilities for these encounters are endless, heartbreaking, confusing and expensive; both for remediation and your anxiety meds. We suggest making friends with a lawyer and stocking the liquor cabinet for off hours. Just to clarify, there are none.

OFFICE MAINTENANCE: Your office in the kitchen and bath should be maintained for efficiency and safety. Constant cleaning is necessary as staff have a tendency to enter main office several times an hour for thirst or sustenance. Ironically, your stainless steel desk will be buried in garbage that no one disposes of while incredibly possessing a garbage disposal. Your satellite offices will need more constant attention as no one who uses them will pay it. Staff trajectory is poor and frequent. Some agencies may show up unexpectedly to inspect said offices. They may even have stopped at closest Sinclair station to use their cleaner facilities before gracing your door. Fortunately they will have ample advice to improve your current chaotic situation as they have drawn a curtain over their own shortcomings.

After their brief stay or a casual critical comment from friends you may want to hit the (no)off hours cabinet. However, some bottles may not have their usual punch as teen staff has diluted them while you were off care-freeing it at the emergency room.

MEDICAL: Medical issues may arise but usually in the middle of the night or while you are out of town as that seems to suit the Laughing Gods of Parenthood. There will be stitches, broken bones and bruises. In a "sugar makes the medicine go down" slip, do not suggest paying a dollar for each stitch as subsequent bleeders will ask the attending for a few extra pricks in which to bleed you dry. Frankly, none of us needs a few extra pricks. Other issues may be on a need to know basis, and usually a teacher, policeman or PPPK will call you if you need to know. Due to a best friend code, which your children signed without your knowledge, you must again smile, nod and look forward to weak vodka. Note: If a staff's toe is amputated due to water balloon fight you instigated, be mindful not to wear wet spandex and a baseball cap covered in whip cream to the Emergency Room. This may result in some loss of respect from professionals as you shiver intensely while consoling amputee. While freezing, attempt to keep your cool when your teen staff burst in to ER with a tip for you in a plastic bag. Also, digits should not be iced and covered in milk regardless of motherhood manuals you have previously read. Although child services is not likely to follow up, your adult cohort may question continued tradition of water balloon fights on last day of school.

RETIREMENT BENEFITS: Not surprisingly, there are no retirement packages offered as this is a permanent position. It is a life-long occupation. You will always be part of the company, and the company part of you. Although you may now enjoy some actual off hours as much of your day- to-day duties subside. As a bonus the liquor and the memories will be stronger. Retirement will be filled with occupiers remnants and enough tiny elementary school pics to wallpaper a small room. Several colorful yet erotic clay images made by tiny hands will show up in every dusty corner. Many more cards, letters, awards and citations (both kind) will fill dozens of plastic totes with lids that don't fit. These are now the things you can worry about instead of money and grades. Neither of which ended up being as important as when the occupation first began. Standing at your desk in the kitchen is also decidedly different once the staff has left the building. It once required two of you to give a fussy toddler a nasty pink antibiotic, which he still spit on the ceiling. Now it may take two of you to open a medicine bottle and that toddler's own child to help read the instructions. While you lost money and promotions were nonexistent and the hours were interminable…the benefits will still far outweigh the hard work. Trust us on this.

Who in their right mind would take on this job? No one and all of us. Our occupying army has grown up in spite of our interventions and set up camps elsewhere. My desk at the kitchen sink is used less often now. No longer are dirty cups and cereal bowls circling my desk as they have been replaced by glaucoma drops and statins. Nothing could replace the thrills of that long roller coaster ride I took hanging bareknuckled on to it's stainless steel sides. It often took nerves of steel and resulted in screams of terror. There were many right turns, a few wrong ones, and massive ups and downs with a few sharp plunges. All in all, a very fun ride. I am now on the down side and my grip is slipping. However, I did learn that one must hold on tight, hit the bar occasionally and occasionally even throw up your hands. This occupation was the ride of a lifetime and I barely even left my office.

EARLY MORNING DRUMBEATS

LYNN STRAND MCINTOSH

It is interesting how a random comment, which all of mine are, can illustrate the difference in how one approaches life. My husband and I march to different drummers, with different strokes and in different bands. However, we are much more in tune with each other at this point in our lives than at any other over the last 45 years. Nevertheless, the way we approach the little things in life still creates amusement.

We were both up at six this morning which is highly unusual for me and I tried to give him his usual peace and quiet. I took the paper to read on our couch. Apparently reading the paper was his next move after reading his emails. We split the paper and he adjusted. Then we had more coffee and watched the finale of Blacklist. It was a lot of blood and gore before seven, contradicted by the safe warm feeling on the couch together. As he showered I collected the trash. By the time he was dressed and in his "moving on" mode he found the trash in the middle of the kitchen floor. I was cooking up expired turkey bacon as he brushed past me picking up the trash. He mused, "Interesting place to leave this". In my mind, I was planning to put the bacon drippings in there when I was done and then move on. I cooked far from perfect eggs in sparse bacon grease and he mused, "That's not the way I would have done it." "No Shit" was my comment. Trash talking finished and a quick disagreement about the heater in the greenhouse and he is ready to leave. I mentioned that I filled up the car the night before for $40 and didn't believe it was full because it was so cheap. Bemused, he looked my way and said, "Just look at the gallons, if it is sixteen it is full." Do we seriously always have to suggest a different way. Then I thought about it and told him the method I have always used to fill up my cars. I just watch the money, and when it dings, I squeeze off a bit more to make the amount end in 0 or 5, I never look at the gallons. His drumsticks are gallons, mine are dollars. The beat goes on.

We could not be more different. It is an inherent difference and one that we are still recognizing. His way of seeing the world and mine are stark opposites. We may not understand each other's views but we have learned to acknowledge and accept it. This truce has taken nearly forty of the last forty five years. I did not drop the trash in the middle of the kitchen floor to piss him off. It was just one of life's little bonuses. We have several of these bonuses every day. I will continue to fill my tank the money way and he can keep making suggestions I will ignore. As long as he makes the coffee and shares the couch we will adjust. After all, we somehow managed to raise five sons who also hear distinct different distant drummers. Our amusing differences make the best music. However, I plan to sleep in tomorrow. Early morning solos are easier on both of us.

A KNOCK AT THE DOOR

DEBBIE PARKER

People often say what they would do if faced with a potentially dangerous situation. Seldom does reality play out the way one expects. My life changed irrevocably with a knock on my front door. The late 1980s may have been last century, but I remember the events of that day as if they happened yesterday.

On a sunny warm summer day, I was pinning a Vogue sun dress pattern onto a piece of cotton fabric when I heard a knock at the door. Even though it was my day off from work and school I was alone, so it startled me. A louder more incessant knock followed the first one. When I looked out the window, I did not see anyone. It was long before the invention of Ring Doorbell, and there was not a peep hole to check.

I opened the door slowly keeping one hand on the door jam. A nondescript man in his twenties who looked a little worse for wear told me that his car had broken down and asked to use my phone. Several thoughts flew through my mind. My parents and Sunday School teachers advised me to help people in distress, so stories of the Good Samaritan competed with the rational thinking of letting a stranger in my home.

While I was vacillating what to do, he followed up with another plea telling me that his car had broken down, and he had to get to work. That made it harder for me to decide what to do. In a similar situation, I would have wanted someone to help me. Remember, it was years before cell phones, so he did not have many options to get assistance.

I looked around and did not see anyone lurking in the area. In a dreamlike state, I nodded okay and moved to the side so he could use the phone which was close to the door. I knew he only appeared to use the phone when I saw that his finger was on the button to disconnect the call. After the ruse, he came into the next room where I was working. I remember clearly every detail that happened after that fake call.

He told me that he could sew better than me. Too late, I quickly realized my error. The nightmare continued. I wanted to appear strong, but I also did not want to enrage him. I slowly looked up, but did not make eye contact with him.

By now, he acted pretty confident and asked to use my bathroom. I told him it was down the hall. I just wanted him to leave as soon as possible, so I agreed in order to get him away from me, the wall phone and the door. As soon as he left, I grabbed the phone and called my husband. I wanted the intruder to know that I was on the phone. I thought that if he knew that I had contacted someone who would help soon. In a calm voice, I greeted my husband loudly enough that the guy could hear me. Then I whispered rapidly in a very shaky voice that there was a man in the house and not to hang up. Shortly after I started talking to my husband, the intruder cheerfully told me, "You're out of toilet paper." I knew that this was not the truth because I had put out a new roll earlier that day.

People often tell you what they would do if they found themselves in a dangerous situation where they fear for their safety, but unless you have experienced a serious trauma, you really do not how you will react. When you are in a situation and you know that you might be hurt unless you protect yourself, you have to make one of the most important decisions of your life. His attempt to draw me into a more isolated part of the house did not work. The fact that he betrayed my trust infuriated me. I immediately went from being the victim to being the one in charge of the situation. I yelled back to him, "I don't think so." At the same time, I reached into the desk drawer that was under the phone and pulled out my dress maker steel scissors. These were not plastic Fiskers with thin metal blades, but rather your grandmother's old-fashioned don't mess with me scissors. Held firmly in front of me with the blades facing out I showed him I would stab him if he dared to touch me.

His cocky smile dropped when he came down the hall and saw the scissors pointed directly at his chest. To prove he had not lost all of his manliness, he regained a little smirk as he hastily made his way to door. Luckily, the phone cord was long enough that I could lock the door once he exited without ending the call. I told my husband that I was safe and to get home quickly. Of course, the last part could have gone unspoken because he got home in record time.

After the culprit left, I felt compelled to see what damage he may done to my home, but I also was afraid to know. I knew that I had to face the scene of his deceit or I would not be able to continue to live here. I slowly went down the hall and into the bathroom where I found the empty paper spool. I glanced around the room and did not see what he might have done with all the toilet paper. I thought that maybe he had taken it with him. I hated to touch anything that I thought he might have handled. When I lifted the lid on the laundry hamper and shoved a few articles of clothing aside, I found the paper wadded up. The next thing I heard was a primal scream, and I found myself rocking back and forth in a fetal position on the floor with tears streaming down my face. At that moment, the adrenaline that had kept me safe left as quickly as it came leaving an exhausted shell.

Because I was in a state of shock, I do not remember getting up off the floor. I staggered back to the living room where I felt slightly safer. I jumped at every noise thinking the intruder may come back. When I heard my husband enter the house, I grabbed the scissors again. He calmed me down enough that I could complete a sentence clearly enough to be understood. We called the sheriff's office and explained the situation. When the two officers came to the door, I panicked again reliving the trauma. The one who took my statement made me feel a little calmer as I explained what had happened, and he took my statement.

Trauma has unexpected consequences. Everything scared me even the other officer who looked around the room made me nervous. The irrational thought going through my head at that time was, "Why didn't I do the dishes this morning. He's going to think I'm a bad housekeeper." I know now that probably I was still in shock and normal thoughts helped me to keep my sanity. Having to relive the trauma was excruciating. I did not think that anything could shock me after this experience. However, the day was full of surprises when the officer told me that a man fitting that description had done something similar a month before and also a week ago. When the deputy told me that the suspect seemed to more brazen with each woman he confronted, my heart raced even faster.

Normally I am a very strong independent woman, but I felt like a child again. I feared every man who came close to me or looked at me for more than a few seconds. I was afraid to be alone again and afraid of every man I encountered. Time and a counselor at the MU Women's Center helped me to heal faster. After two weeks, I checked with the authorities to know if there had been more instances similar to mine. Fortunately, they told me that I had probably scared hm enough that he had not tried anything with another woman.

My world changed that day. It is not something from which I will ever fully recover. I learned many things about myself including not to be as trusting, but still try to help people who truly need assistance. While it is good to have a plan, it is more important to trust yourself to make the right decision. I hope my experience helps others face dangerous situations with courage. Some people say, " No good deed goes unpunished". I disagree. I believe people need to help others just do so with caution.

A LITTLE DIFFERENT

BILLIE HOLLADAY SKELLEY

"I don't even know what that word means," Charlie pleaded.

My six-year-old son had tears swelling in his eyes. I knew he was distressed, but so was I. Was he being truthful this time, or was this just another one of his games? I really didn't know, but I was determined to call the church and figure this one out. This "Charlie episode" could not go unchallenged.

"I am at a loss, Charlie," I told him, "but I'll try to figure it out."

I retreated to my bedroom to regain my composure. Sitting down on the bed, I reminded myself that raising children is a challenge and raising Charlie is an even bigger challenge because he is a little different from other children.

Exasperated, I laid down on the bed. It seemed to me there were always problems where Charlie was concerned. He just wasn't like other kids. Charlie made linkages between words where no one else saw a bond. He made connections where others did not even see a correlation. He just interpreted things differently from other people. Charlie was a good kid, I told myself. He just thinks a little differently.

I also told myself to calm down. After all, it probably wasn't Charlie's fault. Most likely there was some sort of miscommunication at the church, but why, I thought, is there always confusion and misunderstanding around Charlie? Why couldn't he just be normal like other kids?

Tapping my fingers nervously on the bedspread, I thought back to when Charlie was in preschool. He was always exchanging similar sounding words—on purpose. He would say *taste bugs* instead of *taste buds*, *King Solomon's minds* instead of *mines*, and how Jesus was born on a *table* instead of in a *stable*. He understood the actual words and their meanings, but he thought substituting different words made it more interesting and amusing.

Charlie's word substitutions, however, often had been a source of frustration and embarrassment for me. I remembered the time he was in a preschool Thanksgiving play and had insisted on saying *Indians and penguins*, instead of *Indians and Pilgrims*. When the audience laughed at his words, it had been like adding fuel to a fire. When I questioned Charlie why he had said *penguins* instead of *Pilgrims*, he told me the Pilgrims, in their black and white dress, looked like penguins, so he thought of them as being in the same family! I guess there is some logic there, but I just remember feeling embarrassed.

Staring up at the ceiling of my bedroom, I also recalled the tree fiasco in kindergarten.

Charlie's teacher had asked him to thank the Conservation Society for providing a free tree for every child in his class. Charlie did, but he said *Constipation Society*, instead of *Conservation Society*. I remember leaving the room and hiding in the bathroom till the directors of the Conservation Society had left the school.

Rolling over on the bed, I also thought about Charlie's obstinate period, and the antagonistic conversation he'd had with our elderly neighbor when she asked him how old he was.

"I'm four," Charlie told her.

"When will you be five?"

"When I'm done being four," he'd answered.

This had been followed by his literal period.

His kindergarten teacher once said, "Here is your heart," while pointing to a diagram of the human body.

"No," replied Charlie. "That is a poster."

"Well, here is your heart," said the teacher, turning and gently touching Charlie's chest.

"No," answered Charlie. "That's my shirt."

Then he had gone through another strange word substitution phase. Like when he kept referring to Shakespeare as *Jiggleknife*. I had to explain to his teacher that "shaking a spear" was similar to "jiggling a knife," so in Charlie's mind, Shakespeare was *Jiggleknife*!

My face reddened just thinking about the incident at the pediatrician's office.

Charlie had told the pediatrician that I put *gasoline* on his bottom for a rash. He was substituting *gasoline* for Vaseline, but I still worry that pediatrician considers me some kind of abusive parent.

Recalling these memories was not helping me to regain my composure. I told myself to stop reliving the past and to start focusing on today. Charlie's teacher had signed him up for a cognitive assessment test, and now, because of my bedroom retreat, the test was only an hour away. His teacher hoped this test might shed some light on how Charlie thinks. I remained skeptical, but I told myself: *Everything in good order. Today, the school test ... tomorrow, the church.*

Charlie and I drove to the counseling center. Mrs. Larson, the proctor for Charlie's test, told me I could observe through a one-way mirror. I took my place in the darkened room and said a prayer that Charlie would act normal.

Mrs. Larson put a picture of a dog in front of Charlie. The dog, laying on a rug, was curled up and sleeping by a fire.

"What is the dog doing?" Mrs. Larson asked Charlie.

On the other side of the glass, I smiled to myself. This was easy. Charlie will know the dog is sleeping.

"What is the dog doing?" Mrs. Larson repeated.

"He's making a circle," answered Charlie.

In the darkened room, I started to feel frustrated again. Charlie knew the dog was sleeping, so why did he say that? Mrs. Lawson must have read my mind because she asked Charlie to explain his answer.

"Why do you say he is making a circle?" Mrs. Larson asked.

"Because he's curled up on the rug in a circle sleeping," answered Charlie.

"Okay," Mrs. Larson responded. She smiled as she asked, "Charlie, do you know what H2O is?"

"Yes," answered Charlie. "It's a TV station my mother won't let me watch."

"No, Charlie," I moaned softly behind the glass. "She said H2O, not HBO!"

My frustration increased with each additional question. I wanted to scream, *STOP THE TEST! Charlie knows the correct answer, but he's just playing with you.* This time, however, Mrs. Lawson did not read my thoughts, and she continued. "Charlie can you tell me how a yard and a pound are related?"

I knew Charlie would answer this one correctly. We had talked about units of measurement, and he understood how many feet are in a yard and how many ounces are in a pound.

"Charlie," Mrs. Larson repeated, "can you tell me how a yard and a pound are similar?"

"Well," answered Charlie, "if you have a dog, you can put him in a yard or in the pound ... but it's better to put him in the yard because he might get euthanized in the pound."

I closed my eyes. Mrs. Larson continued to ask questions, but I no longer wanted to hear them or Charlie's answers.

Finally, after another hour, the test concluded. Mrs. Larson sent Charlie to play in an adjoining room. When she motioned for me to join her, I did, and I immediately tried to explain that Charlie knew the right answers to her questions.

"Mrs. Larson, I know Charlie didn't do very well on the test, but I assure you he knows many of those answers. Sometimes, he just responds a little differently."

"On the contrary," Mrs. Larson said, "Charlie did very well on the test."

I looked at her with disbelief.

"But he got so many questions wrong," I said.

"There are no wrong answers," Mrs. Larson responded. "The test is designed to show how a child thinks. Sometimes, seeing things a little differently is good. It means a child is taking in information, analyzing the material—often in a unique way—and coming up with his own conclusions."

We talked for half an hour. Mrs. Larson said Charlie was good at *out-of-the-box* thinking, and it's a unique gift. She said being able to see things a little differently can lead to new concepts and ideas and to new discoveries and innovations. I listened to her explanations, and I began to understand that maybe Charlie was different, but being different could be a good thing.

When I left Mrs. Lawson, I still wondered if *normal* thinking might not be easier for everyday life, rather than *out-of-the box* thinking, but it was nice to hear that Charlie's way of thinking, even if it was a little different, could be a positive characteristic.

I retrieved Charlie from the playroom, and we headed home. In the car, I told Charlie that Mrs. Larson said he did well on the test. Charlie smiled at me.

Today's hurdle is over, I thought to myself. *Tomorrow, I will tackle the church.*

The next day, I called the First Baptist Church. The office secretary answered.

"Could you tell me why," I demanded, "on Charlie's Sunday School form, it says he is illegitimate?"

"I don't know," stammered the secretary. "Someone must have provided that information or written it down by mistake."

"Charlie is not illegitimate," I informed her.

"No, of course, he isn't," answered the secretary.

"Well, I'll stop by this morning to make sure the records are corrected," I announced and hung up the phone. I was abrupt, but I was upset again. *Why do these things keep happening?* When we arrived at the church, Reverend Taylor met us.

"I think I know what happened," Reverend Taylor announced.

"I'd like to hear it," I answered.

"Well, I believe when you dropped Charlie off last week to sign up for the first-grade Sunday school class, we had some high school students helping to fill out the enrollment cards. One of the girls, Sandy Warren, remembers talking to Charlie. She asked him where his mother was, and Charlie said she was parking the car. When Sandy asked Charlie where his father was, he told her his father was absent. Sandy then asked Charlie if he meant his father was deceased, and Charlie said *no, he's absent*. Sandy is in the gifted program at her high school. She's very smart, but sometimes she sees things a little differently. Anyway, Sandy assumed Charlie meant his father was not in the picture, so she wrote down *illegitimate* on his registration card."

Turning to face Charlie, I asked him, "Why did you tell that girl your father was absent?"

"Because he wasn't there."

"You never said you were illegitimate?"

"No," Charlie answered. "I don't even know what illegitimate means."

I sighed. Reverend Taylor laughed.

"Charlie, the important thing," said Reverend Taylor, "is for you to remember that you have a father. You also have a Heavenly Father who cares for you very much."

"A Heavenly Father?" questioned Charlie.

"Yes," said Reverend Taylor. "God is your Heavenly Father."

Without missing a beat, Charlie said, "So, I am the son of God."

My cheeks reddened. I could hear Charlie telling everyone he is the son of God.

"Not exactly," I told him.

Reverend Taylor laughed.

"Charlie, I have been saying those words for forty years, and no one has come so quickly to that conclusion." Reverend Taylor looked at me and added, "I hope I didn't make things worse."

"No, Reverend," I answered, "you've helped me to understand something. I'm always seeing Charlie as a challenge ... and worrying whether something is wrong with him, but I think the problem is with me. I need to learn to enjoy Charlie's unique perspective on life. Each day with him is a challenge, but it's certainly never dull. It's always a new trip, and I need to learn to sit back and enjoy the ride."

"I think," said Reverend Taylor, "you and Charlie are going to have a wonderful journey together."

Looking at Charlie, I smiled. "We're going to try, aren't we, Charlie?"

Charlie smiled back at me. "Yes. I like trips," he said. "Can we go to Uranus? I want to see your ..."

"Charlie!" I quickly interrupted. "Let's go home."

SLEEPY

JANA STEPHENS

In downtown Mexico City, five traffic lanes serve buses, cars, commercial trucks, and taxis; the vehicles struggle for position, generating cacophony as they whiz past the Metropolitan Cathedral. It is the the city's grandest treasure, the largest cathedral in all Latin America.

As the street is busy, so, too, is the adjoining wide sidewalk that fronts the cathedral; it swarms with workers and with tourists from many cultures. The cries of street vendors become insubstantial, drowned out by the apparently tireless organ grinders, churning out tune after tune, all loud, and all with a grating sameness.

Amid all the motion and movement, a woman, perhaps twenty-eight years old, stands quite still on the sidewalk directly in front of the cathedral. Her black hair is pulled into a tight braid; her dark blue shirt is tucked into matching pants, and she wears black leather oxfords and belt.

She is an ordinary-appearing woman, but becomes noteworthy because of the yawns, which are enormous: yawn after yawn, again and again. She seems frozen with weariness and doesn't put forth the effort to cover her mouth when it seemingly forces itself open.

Sleepiness has dulled her awareness of her surroundings; the woman's eyes seem to see nothing as she stares into the air immediately in front of her. Each yawn is more substantial than the one before. Her eyes close for several second intervals, but they always pop open. It is imperative that she not fall asleep, for she is one of two Federal Police Officers standing guard at the entry to the cathedral grounds through the tall iron fence. She yawns and yawns. Her eyes close.

THE FINISH LINE

BONNIE ZELENAK

I'm in line for the finish line. I thought it would never be my turn, just like every young, healthy person believes it will never be his or her turn. Mother and Daddy crossed nearly thirty years ago, as hard as that is to believe. Mother was ready. She'd been ready for a long time, having forgotten who she was or what brought her joy. But Daddy wasn't ready. He was her care-giver, and he wasn't going anywhere, not while she still breathed. Mother didn't appreciate him or his loyalty, but she needed him, and that was enough.

Did he know she didn't like him? Hadn't liked him for a long time? He might have, but it didn't matter. "I only want to live a second longer than her," he told me. Perhaps he was making up for past transgressions. Perhaps he simply loved her and always would.

He lasted a year after she passed and toward the end he'd ask, "Where's your mother? I can't find her." He refused to wear hearing aids and he often asked while we were in a restaurant. I'd have to shout the answer, "She's gone, Daddy."

"Well?" He'd ask, looking troubled. He had attended her graveside service, but only saw an urn, not Mother. I had to be blunt or the question would continue, so I told him what he could understand. "She died."

"Yeah?" He'd ask, again wearing a look of surprise. "Did I know that?"

"Yes, Daddy, you came to her service. Want me to take you to the grave?"

"No. I wouldn't want that."

We had that conversation nearly every weekend.

My daddy died eleven months after Mother passed. It happened on my daughter's second birthday. My husband, son, daughter, and I celebrated at Applebee's that night, and we didn't take the time to see Pop Pop. It was late, and she was sleepy when we finished up. Daddy was probably in bed. The nursing home was only fifteen minutes away. But we didn't go.

Not forty minutes after we got home, the call came. "We're sorry, Hon, but your father passed away tonight. When we checked on him, he was gone. He didn't suffer."

"Can I come say goodbye?"

"Not tonight. The ambulance is picking him up soon. Taking him in. You won't be able to see him."

Taking him in? In where? That's Daddy she's talking about. That's Pop Pop. But it didn't matter to her. It was my fault. I should have visited him before heading home. But I didn't. Now, I'd have to wait to see his remains at the memorial home. Before they put him in the incinerator.

When Mother died, I visited her before the cremation. I took in a pretty outfit, and they dressed her in it. I got to say goodbye, and she looked better than she had in years. She crossed the line with dignity.

They didn't ask for nice clothes for Daddy and they didn't let me see him. I had refused a feeding tube for him, and I assume he looked awful. Skeletal. Maybe they were being kind, but I was miserable. They'd bring his remains to the services when they were scheduled, they told me. There was no need to take him home.

Daddy died eleven months after Mother. He wasn't ready to cross the line, not because he wanted to live, but because he was looking for her. Looking for a way to help if she needed anything. In the end, he couldn't swallow, and I'm sure he'd have refused a feeding tube if they'd asked his permission.

He wouldn't have wanted to live with no hope of seeing Mother, so I'm okay with the decision I made. In the end, I helped him cross the line.

My family bought the site where Mother and Daddy reside. They're together in their urns. The wall that houses them is in a sunny spot in the cemetery and they'd have been happy with the location if it were in Pennsylvania, near where they grew up, near a long line of family members.

They're interred here, where I live, and I hope they're okay with that. I won't move them to Pennsylvania and I won't sell their pre-paid plots. Maybe a cousin will want them. Maybe another family member is ready to cross the line. Our extended family has never been close, but those I remember will need plots before long. Hell, I'll need one before long.

My daughter is thirty-two. Her brother is thirty-six. She doesn't think I'm in line. She doesn't think her dad is in line. But her brother knows we are. He knows it's there waiting for us. We had a close-call with my husband a month ago. Without warning, the man who worked out every day, the man with lots of energy, was told he needed trans aortic valve replacement surgery immediately. The day before we planned to fly to Nassau, the cardiologist said he wasn't going anywhere. Two weeks later, I waited in the hospital and worried that his line was approaching too quickly, making its mark. But it's been pushed back. His surgery went beautifully. He was up and walking the next day, feeling better than he had in months. And he continues to improve.

Are we close to the line?

It's getting closer.

It hides beneath the creek at the foot of the hill. It's a breath away. It's at the end of our winding driveway, inching its way toward us. I recognize it, although I pay little attention. My husband might have crossed recently, except for good fortune. We're aware. We're not making plans, but we will. We'll tell our kids where to find relevant documents when it's time. But we'll try not to won't worry them. No need for that. Everybody crosses the line.

FLASH FICTION

Spanish Riviera by Marilyn Hope Lake

FLASH FICTION JUDGE

JENNIFER STEVENS

Jennifer Stevens is a graduate of Montclair State University, NJ. With a bachelor's in English Lit, she's had the privilege of teaching at a small technical college and is a former acquisitions editor at a small press. Writing under three pen names, she has 60 books on the market and has plans to continue writing until she exhausts her ideas--which would be never.

2021 SUMMER FLASH FICTION WINNERS

June
1st Place: [1]Nutso by Terry Allen
2nd Place: Recreating by T. Valleroy
3rd Place: About Van Gogh by Karen Mocker Dabson

July
1st Place: Walking Papers by Liz Yanders
2nd Place: Passage by Nancy Jo Allen
3rd Place: Annabelle and Barney by Terry Allen

August
1st Place: "Jungle Law" by Karen Mocker Dabson
2nd Place: ("Tie) Mystery" by Nancy Jo Allen

Full Circle by Sara Southard
3rd Place:[2]Mere Mortals by Liz Yanders

---

1. *Submission withdrawn from Well Versed 2022.
2. Submission withdrawn from Well Versed 2022

WALKING PAPERS

OVERALL 1ST PLACE; JULY 1ST PLACE

LIZ YANDERS

Mom always said I didn't belong here.
Usually when she put on lipstick
in front of the mirror and left me with her kids
to go out dancing with one of her men

She'd draw the cross across her chest
and repent her sins -- a holy mess.
But I knew there weren't enough beads on that Rosary.
We share the same blood, but she's not me.

She said I deserved better, but smoked cigarettes
and watched TV while I cleaned the toilets.
Said she'd never be pretty, but read Hollywood magazines
while I swept the floor and did the dishes.

I had secrets too. Dreaming underneath an open window,
but laughter and stale whiskey
from the other room blocked the breeze.
Didn't matter, my plans would set me free.

Mom wasn't wise to them until the day she hid my shoes.
Determined not to cut me loose
she said, "You're not going nowhere."
Selfish, ungrateful were her kindest words.

But I stood up on that stage, barefoot.
Clocked my last hour, a graduate.
Threw my cap in the air.
Out the front door with my walking papers.

RECREATING

OVERALL 2ND PLACE; JUNE 2ND PLACE

T. VALLEROY

To create, you must first recreate.

That's what John's mother had said when she'd taught him his pleases and thank-yous, modelling manners. That's what she'd said when she'd put a paintbrush in his toddler hands and shown him Starry Night. He'd spent his younger years copying brushstrokes, mimicking art, and putting on the smiling face he'd seen his mother wear every day, no matter the burden it hid. A person is just a sum of their experiences, afterall, so John took bits and pieces from the world around him, and built himself up.

But then, just when he was sure he'd created a man his mother could be proud of, she was gone.

The world was gray after the funeral. The flowers had lost their splendor, the sun its warmth, and even the creature comfort of a good cup of coffee left the taste of ash in his mouth.

Most days he wanted nothing but to stay in bed and waste the day away.

But he knew it wasn't what his mother would have wanted.

So, one morning, John rolled out of bed, picked up a paint brush, and set to work. The result was clumsy, but it didn't matter. Beauty hadn't reentered the gray world around him, but he could recreate what had brought him joy before, and that, at least, was a start.

FULL CIRCLE

OVERALL 3RD PLACE; AUGUST 2ND PLACE

SARA SOUTHARD

Maritza glanced back at me in the mud, water dripping from the hood of her yellow rain slicker. "You oaf." She offered a hand and I took it. It was a joke between us, my natural "grace," bestowed upon me by our grandfather. He died after tumbling down an embankment. My grandmother said it was poor terrain and bad weather; my great-uncle blamed weak ankles.

Rising to my feet, I immediately leaned against one of the boulders that had tumbled down the hillside, trying to catch my breath. My sister possessed all the desirable physical attributes. I could barely walk on a flat surface without hurting myself. I looked down. "I think we just found it."

I leaned over and brushed mud away from what had tripped me. *April 15th*. It was the stone that marked the place my grandfather was buried. After 50 years Granny wanted him back home. That meant finding the remote place he was buried. They were too poor for Saint Christopher's.

I pulled one of the neon markers from my jacket and stuck it into the soft earth. I looked at my sister, tears ready to spill over. We had never met him. She was thinking of Granny on the mantel. "Let's call dad. Now, we can bring him home."

MYSTERY
AUGUST 2ND PLACE

NANCY JO ALLEN

The trowel plunges soil
striking a hard mass.
The gardener stops to work
the earth with gloved hands
clearing away loam that will support
spring bulbs near the lilies
in that garden plot.
Pulling tangles of Creeping Jenny
aside and lifting hosta leaves,
edges of engraved granite
speak to the her in Spanish:
Established April 15.
But when? A section is scratched away
keeping this secret as well as the question
as to what exactly here was settled.

PASSAGE

JULY 2ND PLACE

NANCY JO ALLEN

Once a bulb
planted in the garden
of my womb,
you emerged gangly and wet,
but stalked out lovely
as a calla lily
that occasionally shows blossoms,
but still withholds that splash of color
until the next cycle
of life—the next passage.
As years faded
you grew taller,
stronger,
more colorful
and you showed impressively
in the larger garden.

Now you have graduated
and will no longer be fenced in,

no longer walk the line,
but cross it,
like a goddess sheds restrictions,
grows in virtue,
love,
fertility
and multiplies.

ANNABELLE AND BARNEY
JULY 3RD PLACE

TERRY ALLEN

Alright, here's another one. This is of our dog Barney, who was a mix with a whole lot of hound in him. He liked to chase rabbits and squirrels. He had a lot of love to give. A big-hearted old boy. And this is a photo of our daughter Annabelle, who was named after her great-grandmother. Anyway, this picture was taken around the time she graduated from high school. As you can see, it was a staged photo that she planned all by herself. It was taken on a country road outside of town, around noon on a spring day, 'cause she wanted the sunlight and the shadows just right. Some people think she's walking toward our home, but we lived in town next to the hardware store that was started by my grandfather and his brother. Anyway, Anna was not only interested in the light and dark in the photo, but she had a lot to say about the meaning of the road and fences and trees, and the colors of everything, especially the yellow line which she said was a symbol of optimism, joy, creativity and the presence of God. All that's true, I guess, but as the years have passed, and I look at the photo now, all I can see is the vanishing point in the distance that she's walking toward.

ABOUT VAN GOGH

JUNE 3RD PLACE

KAREN MOCKER DABSON

I've thought a lot about Van Gogh, You know?
How he could make the heavens glow
Surrounding stars with balls of snow

That hurled across the blue-black sky
Entire galaxies on the fly
So intense in their onward flight
They'd swirl off into the night

I think, "Hey, I could paint like that,"
And poised with palette, I stand pat
Pushing paint on the canvas' flat
But dripping more upon my mat

When time arrests my hand in space
And puts a question in my face
If the stars swirl off into the night
And deprive us of their mighty light,

Wait, what on earth would happen then?
Does a great, thick, horrid dark descend?
A soup of ink that might portend
A night of nights without an end?

I gulp – a ginormous gulp – and then I begin to move my brush again
Because after all, I'm only ten.

JUNGLE LAW
AUGUST 1ST PLACE

KAREN MOCKER DABSON

Rosita felt a tendril of bittersweet twine up her chest when she saw that the creeping vines had nearly concealed the granite block. Soon, no one would be able to read the stone, let alone find it in the tangle of undergrowth that was stealing across the estate. Air escaped her mouth, a harsh barking scoff. She hoped with all her heart that in time, no one would even remember the monstrous hacienda that had burned to the ground.

But she knew they could never forget the travesty that had made room for it. How the big machines had arrived during siesta on a baking hot afternoon. How they had mown down the swaths of lush, green rainforest that embraced the tiny village. How they had flattened the thatch huts that her great-abuelo had helped build. His home. Her home.

Memories scorched her mind. Running for their lives, scooping up children, chasing goats, chickens, and guinea pigs into the forest, trying to save some scraps of the life they had known. All for a monument to what? The colossal greed of the so-called developers.

The granite block lay beneath a stone pillar that marked the drive.

Now, verdant green philodendron and fern shrouded it, too, cracking the mortar, disguising its identity as the jungle – the living, breathing jungle – reclaimed its own. A sly smile slid across Rosita's lips. Fire came to aid the jungle, they say, a lucky lightning strike; or perhaps – she smiled again – a match.

CONTRIBUTORS

Photo Credit: Suzanne Connelly Pautler

Lisa Adams-Lloyd In addition to motherhood, writing and fine art photography, Lisa Adams-Lloyd, is an avid history enthusiast; gathering intriguing tidbits of observation and perplexing paradoxes on a lifelong quest for the interesting and novel. Drawing on her professional experiences in psychology and education, she writes to share and celebrate the unique perspectives she encountered in a community of people from all walks of life. She draws on these experiences for her characters, which play a strong supporting role in the background structure of her work. She lives in Columbia, Missouri with her dearly loved children, husband and two dogs.

Nancy Jo Allen was born and raised in Minneapolis, Minnesota, and now lives in Columbia, Missouri, with her husband Terry and their pup Jayden. Her photos, fiction, and poetry are published in various journals. Included among them are *Well Versed,* * *82 Review, Dime Show Review, Interpretations, Third Wednesday, Firewords, Common Ground, Down in the Dirt,* and *I-70 Review.* Her first poetry collection, *Wrinkles in Time and in Love,* is now available through Kelsay Books, Amazon, and locally at Skylark.

Terry Allen is an emeritus professor of Theatre Arts at the University of Wisconsin-Eau Claire, where he taught acting, directing and playwriting. He is the author of the chapbook *Monsters in the Rain* and the full-length poetry book *Art Work,* which has been nominated for the 2022 Eric Hoffer Book Award. His newest collection of poetry, *Waiting on the Last Train*, will be published in May of 2022. His poems have appeared in many journals, including *I-70 Review, Third Wednesday, Popshot Quarterly, Cloudbank, Into the Void* and *Main Street Rag.*

Yolanda Ciolli is owner and publisher of indie presses AKA Publishing and Compass Flower Press. She is also an editor, layout artist, graphic designer, image specialist, and painter. Prior to starting her publishing career ten years ago, she was owner and operator of a film and digital photo lab for twenty-four years in Columbia, Missouri.

In addition to a lifetime of reading and writing, Yolanda has over thirty-five years experience as a clay artist and photographer. She has been published in multiple editions of Well Versed.

Karen Mocker Dabson's debut novel, *The Muralist's Ghost*, received the 2015 Missouri Writers Guild's Walter Williams prize, second place, which recognizes "research or high literary quality involved in the creation of a major work." Some of her short stories and poems have appeared in the anthologies of the Columbia Chapter of the Missouri Writers Guild and several editions of the *Story Circle Journal*. She has received writing awards from both organizations. She was published in the Mozark Press's 2014 *That Mysterious Woman* and several times in the Columbia Art League's juried *Interpretations* shows and anthologies; and in 2017, won first place for poetry from the Missouri Writers Guild. Dabson, formerly of Columbia, MO, now lives with her husband, Brian, in Durham, North Carolina, and has written two more novels.

Gail Denham. A first in the Miss. yearly contest; several poems in *Quill & Parchment*; ISPS newsletter used poems, as did *Poetic Voices* (Pennsylvania); Denham won 3rd place for flash fiction, Well Versed Contest, plus poems used in their up-coming anthology; Several of Denham's poems used in *Sandcutters* (Arizona); a poem won in Tennessee; placed in *Arkansas Monthly*; Denham's poem, "Cooking Shows" published in *Highland Park* muse; wins in Wyoming newsletter; poems accepted in *Distilled Lives*; *Highland Park* published "Junipers" along with a large photo of Denham's (a juniper of course); BCPA used poems. For over 40 years, Denham has been persistent in sending out poems, short stories, essays, newspaper articles and photos.

Steve C. Friedman has lived in Columbia for more than 20 years. He and his wife Marianne celebrated their 20th anniversary like most people did in 2020 by sheltering in place. One of his great joys in life is spending time with Marianne and his children Kate and Will. He has worked for the University of Missouri for 18 years, and previously worked as a reporter and editor in several Missouri towns (Columbia, Jefferson City, Mexico, Dexter, Jackson, and Cape Girardeau).

Kathy Gan has a collection of her writing that starts from when she was in Fourth Grade. After 35 years of marriage, 25 years of teaching, and coming from a large family, she has a broad range of life experiences to draw from. Her writings express the drama of life with a splash of humor.

Ken Gierke has lived in Missouri since 2012, when he moved from Western New York, where the Niagara River fostered a love for nature. He writes primarily in free verse and haiku, often inspired by hiking and kayaking, while his fondness for love poetry may be explained by the fact that he moved to Missouri to be with the woman he eventually married. His poetry has been featured online by Amethyst Review, Silver Birch Press, and the Ekphrastic Review, and it has appeared in several print anthologies, including three from Vita Brevis Press and one edited by d. ellis phelps.

Anne Gifford moved to Columbia, MO, in 2014 after 28 years in DFW. A retired ICU RN, she has completed five masters and an Ed.D., including an MFA in Creative Writing. She continues to revise her MFA Thesis, "Mary's Diner" for future publication. She's been published in a Fort Worth anthology, *Tarrant County Physician, Fort Worth Star-Telegram*, and CCMWG's *Well Versed*. Sometimes she incorporates her world travels in her writing, such as growing up in Japan and as a nurse in Vietnam. Recent writings include an autobiographical anthology about a mentally ill brother. She continues to serve, and write on her experiences, as a Texas jail "Family Reunification and Reentry" counselor under a Federally Funded 2nd Chance Grant.

Melinda Hemmelgarn is a registered dietitian, and the host of nationally syndicated *Food Sleuth Radio*, which airs on KOPN (89.5

FM), each Thursday evening at 5:00 p.m. She writes poetry to create empathy for the human condition, and promote social and environmental justice.

Thomas Herskowitz is a contributor to Well Versed 2022.

Mary Horner is the author of Strengthen Your Nonfiction Writing, and adjunct faculty in the Communications Department at St. Louis and St. Charles Community Colleges. She is the former managing editor of Journal of the American Optometric Association, and Solutions Magazine. She has written for The Credit Professional, Art Business News, and Decor. Her story, "Shirley and the Apricot Tree" was published in Kansas City Voices in 2017.

Wanita Marie Humphrey lives in Jefferson City, Missouri, with her husband, Glen. She enjoys Spending time with her family and friends, writing, traveling, and going to concerts. While teaching for thirty-one years in Missouri's Public Schools, Wanita was active in the Missouri State Teachers Association and served as state president in 1999. She is a member of Kappa Kappa Iota and PEO, a philanthropic organization dedicated to awarding scholarships to women. What are some of the most interesting things Wanita has done? She was the first girl to take Coaching of Baseball at Missouri University. She has a trophy for winning a late-model stock car race, gone parasailing, and has visited all fifty states. Wanita was excited when her first novel, Only a Moment Ago, was published in October. Find out more about this author at her website at www.wanitahumphrey.com This must be filled in the google address line, not google search.

Lisa Pullen Kent is a member of the Columbia Writers Guild and a contributor to Well Versed 2022.

Marilyn Hope Lake, Ph.D. is an award winning writer, painter, & photographer. Lake writes short fiction, poetry, plays & children's books. She received 1st Place in the 2011 Doris Mueller Poetry &

Prose Contest for her children's story, *Boots–The Black Sheep*. Her children's picture book, Buddy and the Grand Cats sold over 500 copies. A second edition, reformatted for Amazon, TWO CATS AND A DOG, won second prize in the Missouri Writer's Guild President's Contests for Juvenile Books in 2017. Her stories and poetry have won many awards and her poetry and prose have been published in Rock Springs Review, STIR, Well-Versed: Literary Works, the Mizzou Alumni Magazine, and the Gasconade Review, to name a few.

Lynne Jensen Lampe has poems in or forthcoming from *Olney Magazine, Yemassee, Anti-Heroin Chic, The American Journal of Poetry, One*, and elsewhere. Also to come is her chapbook *Talk Smack to a Hurricane* (Ice Floe Press, 2022). She's glad to be writing after years away while working various jobs (teacher, activist, receptionist, newsroom graphic designer), navigating marriage and motherhood, and just being scared of what might come out on the page. A 2020 Red Wheelbarrow Poetry Prize finalist, she lives in Columbia, MO, where she edits academic books and journals. Visit her at https://lynnejensenlampe.com or on Twitter @LJensenLampe.

Alice Landrum is a member of the Columbia Writers Guild and a contributor to Well Versed 2022.

Stephanie Langaker is a member of the Columbia Writers Guild and a contributor to Well Versed 2022.

Virginia Lee is an active reader and writer who loves to imagine scenarios that will entertain and touch the reader, then create the perfect character to tell that story. She's had romances published by Berkley/Jove, and has edited and written for equestrian magazines. She works as a middle school media assistant and is surrounded by books all day; the perfect place to be.

Barbara Leonhard's work is published in *Anti-Heroin Chic, Free Verse Revolution, October Hill Magazine, Vita Brevis, Silver Birch*

Press, Amethyst Review, PhoebeMD: Medicine & Poetry, among others. Barbara won prizes and awards for her poetry in the anthology Well Versed 2021 and Spillwords, where she was voted Author of the Month of October 2021, nominated Author of the Year for 2021, and recognized as a Spillwords Socialite of the Year in 2021. You can follow Barbara on her blog site, https://www.extraordinarysunshineweaver.com.

Marcie McGuire began writing poems and short stories when she was very young but has seldom been brave enough to submit her work for publication. She has worked as a librarian, an English teacher, and an editor. A generalist at heart, she has more projects than she will ever finish in one lifetime and is never bored.

Rod McHugh was born in Los Angeles, California. It was there he commenced his undergraduate education, graduating from high school in 1965. Cramming four years into six, he earned his B. A. from a small private liberal arts college before spending a decade in the work force. He moved to Columbia in 1981 to attend graduate school at MU where he earned his M. A. in History. He stayed on for another five years as a very minor administrator in Jesse Hall. By 1990, he found his niche teaching world history at Hickman High School. Since his retirement in 2014 he has written his first novel. He has been published in multiple editions of Well Versed.

Lynn Strand McIntosh…Feels compelled to write about her memories, her thoughts on family, politics and society in order to clear her thoughts for more storage of the same…the phrase "keep in mind" just doesn't work for her.

Frank Montagnino doesn't take writing (or much of anything else) very seriously. He writes for the fun of it and hopes some of that fun rubs off on readers.

Debbie Parker has had poetry and prose published in a variety of publications including: Well Versed, Hot Flash Mama's, Cougars on the Prowl, Show Me Missouri Women, Healing Talk and other publications. She also taught English to international student at Missouri University for many years.

Suzanne Connelly Pautler first started dabbling with creative writing and storytelling as a child. She currently delights in imaginative play with her grandchildren, including creating stories that traverse to other worlds. She is an avid reader, a researcher of a variety of historical topics, presents historical presentations, and is a genealogy detective. Suzanne and her husband reside in Columbia, Missouri.

Millicent Henry Porter lives and plays in Columbia, Missouri with her husband of fifty years. Contributing to the general chaos of her life are four adult children who now have spouses and families of their own. She is grateful daily for their contagious zest for life and all the fodder they provide to fuel her writer's imagination. This year of uncertainty forced her writing hand to be more productive and finish those marooned and stranded stories. For time waits for no one, not even procrastinating writers. Her work is found in a variety of places including *Well Versed, Rise* and *Interpretations.*

Mary Caitlyn Rodriguez is a member of the Columbia Writers Guild and a contributor to Well Versed 2022.

Margaret Settle is a British exp-pat who has made Missouri her home for the past 25 years. A soon-to-be retired School Psychological Examiner, she is looking forward to spending more time writing about her homeland and her adopted country. She loves to research, travel, and seek out places for inspiration. A first entry and winner in the Ozark Creative Writers in 2021 and a Star letter feature for her short story in Britain the Official Magazine has made her even more determined to begin her writing journey.

Susette V. Shreve is once again a contributing author of the newest edition of the book, Well Versed 2022. A now-retired educator with thirty-two years of experience found a new true love in the form of writing short stories and poetry. She lives in the great state of MO with her cat, Mr. Big, along with her dead and dying plants. She's also an independent traveler and collector of adventures. While not traveling she enjoys time at home with friends and family.

Sharon SingingMoon is a poet and visual artist living in mid-Missouri. Sharon draws inspiration from the natural world and our human struggle to balance mind/body/spirit in the face of our own hubris. In between long hikes and watching the fox family living under the neighbor's carport, she dabbles in screenwriting and is working on a historical fiction YA novel. Sharon has a Master's degree in Public Administration and worked as a lobbyist for social justice issues, spearheading several progressive advancements in Missouri before retiring to garden, write and travel. Sharon's work has been published in Interpretations, multiple editions of Well Versed anthology, & Silver Birch Press. Her recent poetry collection, *Random Seed*, can be found at independent bookshops across the mid-West

Billie Holladay Skelley received her bachelor's and master's degrees from the University of Wisconsin-Madison. Now retired from working as a cardiovascular and thoracic surgery clinical nurse specialist and nursing educator, she enjoys focusing on her writing. Billie has written several health-related articles for both professional and lay journals, but her writing crosses several different genres and has appeared in various journals, magazines, and anthologies in print and online—ranging from the *American Journal of Nursing* to *Chicken Soup for the Soul*. An award-winning author, she has written eight books for children and teens—including *Ruth Law: The Queen of the Air* which was selected to receive the 2021 American Institute of Aeronautics and Astronautics (AIAA) Children's Literature Award.

Sara Southard is a graduate of the University of Missouri-Columbia. She began writing as a child and has dabbled in everything from ghost stories to angsty teenage poetry to highly dramatic fan fiction. These days she mostly sticks to fantasy and sci-fi with a particular passion for YA. She lives with her partner, sister-in-law-ish, a sassy tiny human, a big slobbery dog, three exasperating cats and a partridge in a pear tree.

Jana Stephens is a retired RN and lives in Columbia, Missouri. Her writing focuses on rural southern Missouri during the first half of the twentieth century, as well as on her travels in Mexico with extended stays in Mexico City.

Mike Trial is a member of the Columbia Writers Guild and a contributor to Well Versed 2022.

T. Valleroy is a graduate student and author from Missouri, studying in Michigan. They write in the fantasy genre and hope to publish novels in the future.

Liz Yanders' screenplays, *Flint Hill* and *Widow Sims*, have won honors in notable screenwriting contests, including Top Ten ISA Table Read My Screenplay, Finalist WeScreenplay, and Second Rounder Austin Film Festival. Her poems and short stories are published in anthologies, and she occasionally writes movie reviews for an online site.

Lori Younker has made warm and woodsy Missouri her home for over 20 years. Upon her return from missionary work in Mongolia with her family, she found writing a solace and her passion. Currently, she is an English teacher in Mexico Public Schools, where she enjoys teaching reading and writing. In her free time, she shares her home in many forms of hospitality and assists international students at the International Community Church of Columbia, MO.

Bonnie Zelenak enjoys writing short stories, flash fiction, and novels, often with a romantic theme. After thinking about writing children's stories for thirty-plus years, she finally got out pen and paper (AKA her laptop), joined CCMWG, and dug in. She has spent countless hours enjoying the art of learning, sometimes believing she's made progress, sometimes not. Bonnie and her husband live on the outskirts of Columbia and thoroughly enjoy spending time with one another, family, and friends.

Photo Credit: Karen Mocker Dabson

COLUMBIA CHAPTER OF THE MISSOURI WRITERS' GUILD

2021/2022 Board:
President: Deb Sutton
Vice President: Lisa Adams-Lloyd
Secretary: Barbara Harris Leonhard
Treasurer: Charles Tutt
Membership Chair: Anne Gifford
Administrative Secretary/Well Versed Editor: Marsha Posz; (2022)
Administrative Secretary: Lachlan Smith
Member at Large: Frank Montagnino

Quarterly Readings: Sharon SingingMoon and Barbara Harris Leonhard

Flash Fiction Coordinator: Anne Gifford

ACKNOWLEDGMENTS

Photo Credit Debbie Parker

We would like to express our appreciation to everyone who has helped with Well Versed 2022, including our contributors, volunteers, judges, editors, and sponsors.

Images of artwork used in Summer Flash Fiction contest printed with permission form the following:
June prompt-Artist at easel by Bob Seaman
July prompt-New graduate on road by Michelle Scott Huffman.
August prompt-Engraved stone by Joey Edwards..

Well Versed Judges:
Poetry: Walter Bargen
Nonfiction: PoetryDonna Duly Volkenannt
Fiction: Gregory Ashe
Flash Fiction: Jennifer Stevens

Well Versed Volunteers:
Charles Tutt
Lisa Adams-Lloyd
Cortney Danials
Sharon SingingMoon
Karen Mocker Dabson
Deb Sutton
Drew Van Dyke
Lori Younker
Millicent Henry
Liz Yanders
Anne Gifford
Chinwe Ndubuka

Photo Credit: Chinwe Ndubuka

ARTWORK AND PHOTOGRAPHY
MEMBER SUBMISSIONS

Photo Credit: Debbie Parker

A Wish photo by Lisa Adams-Lloyd
Burr Oak photo by Lisa Adams-Lloyd
Marbella Spain photo by Terry Allen
Glendaloch photo by Terry Allen
Nobody Home painting by Dorothy Canote
Butterfly on a flower photo by Karen Mocker Dabson
Curtain at Window photo by Gail Denham
Spanish Riviera painting by Marilyn Hope Lake
Flower in the Rock photo by Chinwe Ndubuka
Outside blue door photo by Debbie Parker
Inside restaurant photo by Debbie Parker
Canyon photo by Suzanne Pautler
Rock formation photo by Suzanne Pautler

Made in the USA
Coppell, TX
30 June 2022

79440359R10164